MW00813248

Endorsements

"This is a book to savor…taking each page as if it were a delicious morsel ready to nourish your soul. This is one of the most truthful books I have read in a long, long time. It doesn't seek to impress. It seeks to teach in a gentle, compassionate way. Michael is walking his talk on every page. As a result, and if we are willing to take it in, we are all made better for it." *Maria Nemeth, PhD, master certified coach and author of* **The Energy of Money** *and* **Mastering Life's Energies**

"In *Loved beyond Measure,* Michael Moran explores the life journey that can take us from feeling awful to awe-filled. He shares his own story about being an angry teen who seemed determined to self-destruct and the awakening that transformed him into a tircless advocate for peace. Michael shares stories about people and events that helped him see that life's greatest blessings so often begin as life's greatest nightmares. This book is filled with insight, humor, and inspiration. Read it and live it." *Tom Zender, bestselling author of* **One-Minute Meditations at Work**, *president emeritus of Unity, professional mentor*

"*Loved beyond Measure* is filled with spiritual wisdom, inspirational hope, and heart-warming stories that reveal how we can each learn to grow from our challenges, live life to the fullest, count our many blessings, and remember to laugh often—with ourselves and others. Michael Moran speaks with authenticity and compassion, as he generously offers us a window into his expansive life of love, passion, purpose, and service. I highly recommend this uplifting and motivational book." *Rev. Vicky Elder, Unity of Monterey Bay, Monterey, CA*

"This is an earthy, common sense book of wisdom that will make you laugh with its honesty and love of life. Out of his pain and loss of the love of his life, Michael Moran has written a gem that will uplift your spirit. The stories are heartwarming lessons from the life of a minister who has become a mentor. They were life-changing for him and will be for you! If you wish to grow spiritually, this is a must-read!" *Rev. David Thompson, PhD, The Interfaith Experience, Sacramento, CA*

"What matters to you? If you're asking, 'Is this book going to make a difference in my life? Am I going to be spending quality time reading *Loved beyond Measure?*' My answer to you is an unequivocal, 'Absolutely yes!' After finishing it, you may want to go back and reread it, underlining particular passages, dog-earing pages, squeezing a little more value from these beautiful, suggestive narratives. I can promise you this book is going to make an impact on your life." *From the foreword by Mary M. Morrissey, author of two best-selling books,* **No Less Than Greatness** *and* **Building Your Field of Dreams**

"Reading *Loved beyond Measure* is like sharing a cup of coffee with Michael Moran. He writes as he speaks in a casual, intimately conversational way. The wisdom he shares from the ups and downs of his own life, plus his extensive studies of world religions and cultures, is timely, relatable, and practical. It's the kind of book you can pick up and flip to any message and find yourself laughing, nodding in agreement or brushing away a tear. One thing for sure: when you reach the last page, you will know you are loved beyond measure." *Rev. James Trapp, senior minister, Spiritual Life Center, Sacramento, CA, past president and CEO of Unity Worldwide Ministries*

LOVED
BEYOND
MEASURE

*Messages of
Inspiration, Hope and Joy*

by
MICHAEL T. MORAN

Edited by Leslie W. Leggio

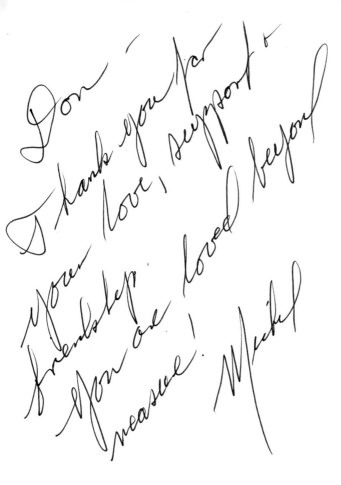

www.OnenessMinistries.com

Loved Beyond Measure

First Edition
ISBN: 0-9891-9510-4
ISBN 13: 978-0-9891951-0-2

Dedication

This book is dedicated to all those who have shared their stories with me over the years; and to Faith Moran, who saved me from myself. She was my Anam Cara, best friend, lover and wife. She demonstrated with her life what real love looks, feels, and acts like.

Michael and Faith Moran

I slept and dreamt that life was joy,
I awoke and saw that life was service,
I acted and behold service was joy.
Rabindranath Tagore

Table of Contents

Foreword

I have known Michael Moran for many years. In these decades, I have come to respect and revere him as an exceedingly fine minister, a joke-teller without peer, a deep thinker, a community leader and healer, and a dear friend. He has been through "the fire"; he walks his talk, and he is truly one of the great people on this planet.

None of that, however, matters to you, the reader. Chances are you may never have the privilege of meeting Michael to know for yourself any of the truth of the above paragraph.

What matters to you? "Is this book going to make a difference in my life? Am I going to be spending quality time reading *Loved beyond Measure?*" My answer to you is an unequivocal, "*Absolutely yes!*"

This is a book of stories in short essay form. They are stories about events in Michael's life, and they all make for truly interesting and captivating reading, but they are far more than mere stories. These are "instructions." Each chapter is a guide to how you can live your life more fully and with greater joy, compassion, and difference-making.

This is also a book filled with amazing quotes. Reading the quotes alone would be worth the price of the book. There are very few volumes anywhere that will give you as much deep joy and appreciation as *Loved beyond Measure*.

Michael was a very popular radio broadcaster in his earlier adulthood. He still has that incredible "radio voice"—deep, resonant, and powerful. As I read these stories, I can *hear* his voice. Imagine, as you read *Loved beyond Measure*, that he is speaking to you, giving you his best advice, amusing you, touching your heart, telling *you* these lessons he has learned and sometimes struggled to know so he could give them to you and me.

After finishing it, you may actually want to go back and reread it, underlining particular passages, dog-earing pages, squeezing a little more value from these beautiful, suggestive narratives. I promise you this book is going to make an impact on your life.

In conclusion, I'd like to do something that is rarely done in a foreword. I'd like to *thank* Michael Moran for making this book available to us. There are some personal revelations that were difficult for him to write, but they help us deal with our own personal struggles. There are some deep universal principles that, when read in more abstract terms, might mean little to us, but, when taken in as part of one of Michael's stories, become immediately clear, usable, and liberating for us.

Loved beyond Measure is about love, and compassion, and judgment, and karma, and self-appreciation, and prayer, and many, many other everyday real-life topics. And even though it was written from the perspective of Michael Moran's life, it's really about your life and my life.

So, thank you, Michael Moran, for creating one of the most wonderful books I've ever read.

In *Loved beyond Measure,* you will find an easy-to-follow, practical guide to your own "well-lived life."

Mary Morrissey
Author, *Building Your Field of Dreams*

Preface

In 2004, my wife, Faith, was diagnosed with posterior cortical atrophy (PCA), a rare neurological condition for which there is no cure or treatment. The news was devastating, and our lives turned upside down immediately. From that diagnosis on, nothing would ever be the same. We began a four-year journey on a roller-coaster ride that plunged us into devastatingly painful and confounding lows and then would catapult us to unimaginable highs of spiritual insight and wonder. As I watched my beautiful wife's mind dissolve and disappear a millimeter a day for years, I questioned every stubbornly held or sacred belief about life, fairness, justice, family, purpose, and God. Nothing went unquestioned.

My whole life revolved around Faith and our love relationship, partnership, and marriage. I adored her, and we were together almost every moment of every day during our twenty-seven years together. We truly enjoyed each other's company. We had experienced great happiness and success in each of our New Thought Unity ministries for over twenty years. We were literally living the life of our dreams and loving it. New Thought offers a positive, practical, and life-affirming approach to spirituality. One of the basic tenets of Unity is called the Law of Mind Action, which states "thoughts held in one's mind produce after their kind." This belief predates New Thought and is a foundation in both Hinduism and

Buddhism. The Buddha said, "The mind is everything; what we think we become."

That belief helped shape the life we were living and is also what made the journey we found ourselves on so frustrating and faith-challenging. The physical mechanism we need to organize and control our thoughts, the brain, was the organ that was fatally compromised. Faith's brain was slowly dying, and her ability to reason, choose, and organize thoughts diminished each day. Her mind was perfect, but she could not hold the images, thoughts, and ideas that she had successfully used and taught all her life, and that had blessed so many people. In the early stages, this irony was not lost on her, and I would watch her struggle to stay focused and positive, which had been second nature for her until then. This is when I started questioning everything I had ever read, believed, taught, and defended. I didn't know what I believed anymore.

Faith's deteriorating condition soon became obvious to our large, interfaith spiritual community. She could no longer speak in complete sentences; she developed tremors and had difficulty focusing. She loved our community and was greatly loved in return. The most difficult day for us was when she had to accept she could no longer serve in ways she had done so effortlessly for two decades. One Sunday I stood beside her at the podium and pointed to words on her script when she got lost. In her halting speech, she informed the congregation, *"I have received the diagnosis from the Mayo Clinic. It is not the one I wanted. People keep asking me, 'Why you, Faith? How could this happen to you? Where did this come from?' These are all the wrong questions. At this point it doesn't matter why or where or how. All I know is this washed up on my beach, and now it is mine to deal with. The only question before me today is, Who do I choose to become as I walk this new path life has placed before me? Please send me your faith, but not your fear, as Michael and I walk this new way."*

As word of Faith's illness spread, thousands of messages of well-wishes poured in from all corners of the earth. Faith, in her humble and joyous manner, had touched many lives in ways she never imagined. These well-wishes and expressions of love enfolded us as we moved along on our new journey of faith. They came from Christians, Jews, Muslims, Hindus, Buddhists, and Pagans. Many asked to be kept updated on our journey. As Faith was slowly disappearing, I started writing a weekly message to keep everyone informed of her condition. These weekly messages became my way of dealing with all the questions that arose as we journeyed together. Thanks to the Internet, people forwarded some of my messages to friends around the world. One lady wrote me on a day when I was at one of my lowest points. It was a beautiful message from someone I had never met, and yet she managed to say just the words I needed in order to get up and face another day. She had signed off, "Never forget you and Faith are loved beyond measure."

I adopted her salutation for my weekly messages, and it seemed to be the natural title for this book. Remember, *you* also are loved beyond measure.

Michael Moran

Acknowledgments

I believe that no matter where we find ourselves in life, we are there by Divine Appointment. This does not mean that there is an invisible force moving us around on a cosmic chess board; it means that no matter where life takes us, there is something we can either contribute or receive. We are always standing on Holy Ground. I have been incredibly blessed in this life to have had a wide variety of experiences, some of which sent me soaring to sublime heights and others that sent me careening into the darkest depths of despair and disillusionment. From where I stand today, I bless them all and thank God for my life.

In my search for Truth, many people came along at just the right time to offer me insight and inspiration or to reveal those uncomfortable parts of me that needed "tweaking." The wisdom shared by many great souls, such as that radical Rabbi Jesus, The Buddha, Yogananda, Meister Eckhart, Ralph Waldo Emerson, Charles and Myrtle Fillmore, Emma Curtis Hopkins, and Pierre Teilhard de Chardin, expanded the horizons of my life and my concepts of the Creative Force we call God.

I offer my sincerest gratitude to all the people who have touched me at depth and helped shape me into the person I still endeavor to become. I am especially thankful to my family and many friends who have born witness to the best and worst of me over the years. As my late wife's long illness progressed, my walking partners Mike Zeglarski, Mary Worrell, and Leslie Leggio ("the peeps") helped keep me grounded and sane on those 5:00 a.m. walks each day. We pretty much shared every detail of our lives, which means we can never stray far from one another. Many of the stories in this book had their genesis on those walks.

Leslie Leggio not only walked with me, she encouraged me to write this book and, in her typical fashion, offered to tangibly support me each step of the way. She not only became one of my dearest friends and trusted confidant, she is also my business partner in Oneness Ministries and the editor of this book. Thank you, Les.

Faith, my cherished Anam Cara, wife, and lover, made me want to be a better person. She showed me, by the way she lived her life, what Big Love looks and feels like. I definitely got the best end of that deal.

To all the authors, friends, heroes, and "villains" of my life so far, I want you to know that "you are loved beyond measure."

Michael Moran

Why Are We Here? Becoming Your Best You
The Value of Intention

"What God intended for you goes far beyond anything you can imagine."
Oprah Winfrey

About thirty years ago, I spent New Year's Eve in a cozy cabin in Gig Harbor, Washington. I was alone, unhappy, and unfulfilled. My long-term relationship with a woman had just ended, and I wasn't feeling very good about myself or my life. My career was back-sliding, and I felt I was pretty much a pathetic wreck on every level. All I knew was that I didn't want to show up in the New Year the same way I had been showing up in years past. I took an honest inventory of my character that night and consciously chose to change some aspects that were not serving my Highest Self. I listed them on my legal pad, said goodbye, crumpled up the paper, and ceremoniously tossed it into the fire with a heartfelt "good riddance!"

I then asked God to show me the person I was meant to be. I asked to be shown how I could serve God better. I knew if I was going to authentically change, I had to take total responsibility for my life—no more scapegoats, whining, or excuses. Images began to float into my mind. I visualized the person I wanted to be; the healthy, passionate, committed, holy relationship that my heart of hearts desired to have; and the career path that would serve my soul. I thought of the people I most admired and listed their special qualities.

Next, I did something I have never done before. I wrote a thank-you letter to God as if it were a year in the future. I was writing to express my sincerest gratitude for all the good that had come into my life and for the Divine Wisdom and strength I had received when life took jolting, unexpected turns. The God (concept) I wrote to was not the Scary Old Man in the sky or Santa Claus (God of childhood). It was an available wise mentor, an elder friend who cared about me, loved me unconditionally, and was always there for me when I needed guidance. That was the energy I wanted to tap into.

I cried as I wrote that long letter of thanks because, more than anything, I wanted to be that person I had gratefully described. I wanted to have the life partner with whom I could love and serve. I wanted to feel good about myself and live a life that mattered. I didn't give thanks for things or money; I thanked God for the power to change into that person. I had no idea how I would do any of this, but I trusted my wise mentor, elder friend, God, to show me the way to a life worth living. That mystical night changed the course of my life, and, within a year, my life was starting to look very different. I was slowly becoming the person who just a year before lived only in my mind and on a yellow legal pad.

Three decades later, I am still working on becoming the person I described that night. I have accepted that I am always a work in progress, but that is life. I am mindful of the progress I have made and the many times I still get off course. The difference is now I am able to correct more quickly instead of mindlessly continuing the same old story.

This year, do it differently. What is done is done and cannot be changed, but what stretches out before us is wide open with possibility. Get clear about what is not working in your life. We have the power and the responsibility to change attitudes, habits, and activities that are not serving our soul's growth. Ceremoniously list the things that no longer work for you and release them. Then gratefully and mindfully begin to get crystal clear about who you want to be at the end of this life's journey and how you want to be remembered.

Write your letter to God/Goddess/Higher Power/Divine Presence and tap into the energy that will work through you to do a "life makeover." Be the person God created you to be. Be the great soul you truly are. Let God lead you in all matters and all that matters.

Here is one of my favorite scriptures from the prophet Jeremiah.

"For surely I know the plans I have for you—plans for your welfare not for harm, to give you a future with hope. Then when you call upon me and come and pray, I will hear you."

That is the voice of the Inner Power that will help you make this year a year that matters.

January 2008

"We spend January 1ˢᵗ walking through our lives, room by room, drawing up a list of work to be done, cracks to be patched. Maybe this year, to balance the list, we ought to walk through the rooms of our lives...not looking for flaws, but for potential."

Ellen Goodman

The Gift of Kindness

"Forget injuries, never forget kindnesses."
Confucius

A few years ago the Associated Press released a poll that showed over 70 percent of the American people felt, as a society, that we are ruder and less civil toward each other than we were twenty years ago. The examples given were people talking loudly on cell phones in public places, foul language, and an unwillingness to assist someone in need. I tend to agree with the general assessment of the results, but I still see plenty of evidence of those who keep the flame of kindness glowing.

Recently, I observed a man intently watching an elderly gentleman and his frail wife as they tried to get their bearings in a large warehouse store. It seemed he was trying to decide how to help the couple without intruding on them or bruising their dignity. His face reflected concern and empathy as if he was seeing his parents in the disoriented couple. Just as I was going to offer assistance to the couple, he reached out to them. He casually pretended to be shopping nearby, stopped by the elderly man, and began a light-hearted conversation about how these big stores confused him and he always got lost. The elderly gentleman agreed, and they started talking. The next thing I knew they were laughing, chatting amiably, and comparing shopping lists. The three of them walked off together like old friends as they helped each other find the items on their lists.

I felt warmth in my heart as I witnessed this simple act of selflessness and compassion. The man's act of kindness made me want to express more goodness and common courtesy to the people in my world of influence.

The main reasons I fell so deeply in love with Faith were her "core goodness" and desire to be of service to others. She was the director of the Sunday school at the church I attended with my young daughter, Jennifer. I was a recently divorced "weekend" dad, and Jen was nervous about being separated from me, especially in a strange place.

As I took Jennifer back to the Sunday school area for the first time, Faith, wearing a cheery rainbow apron, greeted her with her signature huge smile and complimented her on how pretty she looked. I noticed this was how she embraced all the new children and their nervous parents. I liked and trusted her immediately.

Faith reached into her pocket, pulled out a magic marker, and asked Jenny if she liked to color. Jen shyly nodded, and Faith said, "Oh, good, because I need some help filling in letters on a sign, so I want you to be my helper and stay right by my side today. You are the answer to my prayer; will you help me?"

Suddenly Jenny went from frightened, awkward child to enthusiastic helper. She let go of her tight grip on my hand and went right to the nice lady with the dazzling smile. She stuck to Faith like glue, and every weekend when she was with me she wanted to go to Sunday school because she was Faith's special helper. Faith made her feel wanted, worthy, and of value, and isn't that what we all desire? It was her genuine kindness and the empathy Faith showed toward everyone that initially turned me on to this remarkable woman with whom I shared life for twenty-seven years.

Begin to take notice of the kindnesses and gentle mercies you observe every day and add to them by being kind and civil to everyone within your circle of influence. Acknowledging kind acts that you witness also encourages others to be kind. Gandhi said, "What you consistently look for and focus on will expand in your life." If you want more kindness, be more kind.

January 2009

"Let no one ever come to you without leaving better and happier. Be the living expression of God's kindness: kindness in your face, kindness in your eyes, and kindness in your smile."

Mother Teresa

The Second Agreement

"Expecting life to treat you well just because you are a nice person is like expecting an angry bull not to charge you because you are a vegetarian."

Shari Barr

Faith and I had an interesting thing happen one day as we picked up a prescription at Rite Aid. When we came back to the car, our battery was dead. I am prepared for these little setbacks, so I pulled out my handy-dandy jumper cables and waited for the person parked next to me in the big red truck, with the meanest little yappy dog I've ever seen, to come out of the store. As the owner approached, I asked with my most pleasant voice and friendliest smile, "Hey, would you mind giving me a jump?" Without even looking at me he said, "No, I don't want to." That was it— no excuse...not even, "Sorry, I'm in a hurry." He brushed past me, climbed into his behemoth truck with the snarling little monster, and drove away. I felt stunned by his abruptness and a little foolish standing there with jumper cables dangling from my hands. I actually took it a little personally, thinking, *what's wrong with me?* Ah, the old familiar ego rears its pointy little head.

I was feeling a little gun-shy about asking someone else, and, as I scanned the area looking for a Good Samaritan, all I could see were women. I usually don't approach women in parking lots because I don't want to put them in an awkward position, but a pleasant woman looked my way and asked, "Do you need some help?" She kindly drove over and gave me the jump I needed and restored my faith in humanity. Also, the good thoughts I had about her cancelled out my thoughts I had about you-know-who and his evil little minion. (I'm just joking here; I'm sure he is a very nice man who was just having a bad day or perhaps not feeling well. I'm not so sure about the snarly little dog.) Perhaps my unkind thoughts about his dog set up the rejection!

As I reflected on my experience and the fact that I took the abrupt rejection so personally, I had to laugh at myself because up until that moment I was having a great day. I immediately remembered Don Miguel Ruiz's powerful book *The Four Agreements*. Agreement number two is "Don't take anything personally." Let's face it—there is an awful lot of negative energy in the world and more than enough people willing to share it with us. If I had chosen to hang on to the experience, I would have kept the poison of his words and abruptness inside me and likely passed it on to others. It's important to remember that what anybody thinks about us or says about us (positive or negative) is more about them than it is about us. By not taking everything so personally, we allow ourselves to be in relationship with anyone and not get trapped in their stuff. Besides, if I am going to focus energy on anyone, it should be the woman who took the chance to help someone out. Life is a great school with many excellent teachers and numerous opportunities to practice growing our souls. After all, that is the only reason we are here.

November 2006

"One should never do wrong in return, nor mistreat anyone, no matter how one has been mistreated by the other."

Socrates

What Do You Mean, "It's All about Me"?

"Blessed are we who can laugh at ourselves, for we shall never cease to be amused!"

Author unknown

One chilly fall morning I was walking with a close friend with whom I can be totally transparent. This is a great blessing in my life, and it has been earned by us over many years, hundreds of hours, and thousands of miles spent walking, talking, or just being silent with each other. With my walking partners, I have learned I don't have to worry about thinking out loud or saying something that will be used against me at a later date. It is a precious gift, like a beautiful pearl, that can only be created over time. It takes a long time to grow an old friend, and I do not take her friendship for granted.

On this particular morning I was describing an opinion or observation a spiritual mentor had shared about me that made me uncomfortable and a wee-bit irritated. My friend listened until I had reached the end of my story and said, "Hmm, doesn't that sound vaguely familiar?" I had no idea what she meant, so I asked, "How so?" My friend replied, "Aren't the words he used to describe you in that situation almost identical to the ones you used to describe someone else just last week?" Arrrgh! She had nailed me but good; I laughingly bopped her on the head with my plastic water bottle and said, "I hate you!"

What I had unconsciously done was a textbook example of what Freud called "psychological bias or projection." I had transferred what I considered unhealthy or undesirable traits within myself, which I had not yet acknowledged and come to terms with, onto someone else. I could easily see within him the traits and tendencies I was not yet willing to deal with in my own life. My friend lovingly and humorously brought this to my attention.

In his book *A Life of Being, Having, and Doing Enough*, Wayne Muller writes, "I always find myself confessing that I could never live deeply, authentically, or well without the close company of my good and loyal friends. They are clear mirrors. By this I mean they understand and reflect back to me my particular strengths and my more challenging weaknesses. They know when I need tenderness and when I need scolding, and they are never reluctant to provide either one. It is their unconditional love and support that enables me to get up in the morning."

My first New Thought teacher said something I have never forgotten. "Try to speak as if this was true; that the words you use to describe another person will be the exact words someone else will use to describe you." She continued, "Words are one of the most powerful tools in the Universe; they can be directed to offer faith, or fear, healing or wounding, life or death, and they produce after their kind. Think before you set that powerful, creative force in motion." I have thought of her challenge many times over the years when I have been tempted to speak words that are less than kind about a person or not beneficial to them. This doesn't mean we can't make honest observations or assessments about someone when necessary, but we want to be very clear about our intentions and agenda before we set the words loose.

There is an adage that states before we speak of another we should first consider whether what we are about to say is "true, kind, and necessary." That is a good rule of thumb, but sometimes life forces us to speak to some unpleasant realities about someone that may not seem to be "kind," at least in the sweet and pleasant way. Another definition of "kind," which I think is better suited, is "being understanding and humane." My kind friend showed understanding and diplomacy when she used gentle humor as an effective means to reveal something I was missing about myself. I looked into the mirror she held up and had to laugh. It was so obvious. How could I have missed it?

If you consistently see someone in a negative light, stop to think for a moment and ask, "Am I projecting?" Also understand that often when someone is criticizing you, they may well be criticizing a projection of themselves. Honestly ask yourself, "Does this have anything to do with me?" If it does, acknowledge and deal with it. If not then remind yourself, "What someone thinks of me is none of my business" and move on. Life gives us many opportunities to look into the mirror of truth.

October 2011

"How far you go in life depends on your being tender with the young, compassionate with the aged, sympathetic with the striving and tolerant of the weak and strong. Because someday in your life you will have been all of these."

George Washington Carver

Respect for Everyone

"Do not wait for your leaders; do it alone, person to person."
Mother Teresa

One day I made an early-morning run to Home Depot to buy bags of bark to spread in the backyard before the day became superheated. I was already hot and starting to get a little cranky. I was loading the bags into the trunk of my car when a scruffy-looking young man approached and asked if I could spare a dollar or two for some food. I automatically replied no, and he "puffed up" and started doing a tough-guy walk, mumbling profanities at me under his breath. I thought to myself, *well, he could have at least offered to help me load the heavy bags into my car for a buck or two.*

Something about the exchange troubled me, though—it wasn't that I didn't give him the money because I often do so when I feel the inner nudge. It wasn't that he had asked me in the first place or cursed at me. It was the fact that I could tell his pride, which was already wounded, had been further damaged by my abrupt response.

I watched the young man approach others until he met a woman who handed him some money as she walked into a coffee shop. He immediately started walking quickly toward a McDonald's a few blocks away. I watched him and remembered a story about my father, who had been the executive director of a Veterans Administration Hospital. One of his department heads had fired a man in a publicly humiliating way, and my father called the manager on the carpet, reportedly saying, "I agree the man deserved to be fired, but no one should have his dignity taken from him." My dad had the manager call the man he fired and offer him an apology and another chance. Both men remained faithful employees for many years.

With that story in mind, I drove to McDonald's and pulled into the parking lot at the moment the young man arrived. He saw me driving toward him, and I could see him start to "puff up" again. I rolled down my window and said, "I apologize for being disrespectful to you; I'm just having a bad day. Let me buy you breakfast." I could see him soften, and we smiled at each other. He replied, "That's okay, thanks man." I felt better, he felt better. The world felt kinder. We both had a little more faith in the human condition.

Today, treat everyone you meet with kindness and courtesy, even those who are rude to you—not because other people are nice or not but because you are.

"If you want to make others be happy, practice compassion; if you want to be happy, practice compassion."

The Buddha

Extending Yourself to Others

"Sometimes being a friend means mastering the art of timing. There is a time for silence. A time to let go and let people hurl themselves into their own destiny. And a time to pick up the pieces when it is all over."

Gloria Naylor

I became deeply aware of the value of friendship one year when I lost two close male friends within three months, Reverend Rory Elder and Ken Swinford. As is often the case, I didn't realize how much I loved and valued them until they were gone. Rory was like a soul brother to me. Ken was like an older brother who prodded me now and then and felt like a thorn in my side at times but never once failed to show up when I needed him. My friendship with Ro was an easy one; with Ken it was a bit more challenging, as we were very alike in some uncomfortable ways. Ro and I would just laugh at each other when we got sideways with one another; Ken and I would butt heads and debate and eventually laugh. With both of these men I could just be me. Sometimes that is risky for a minister because many people have such high and unrealistic expectations of ministers to be everything but human—and, man, am I human!

What made these two men so important to me? They both had the beautiful gift of extending themselves so naturally to others. I used to marvel at the ease with which they encountered other people and made them feel like lifelong friends from the get-go. They were serious, too—it wasn't just an act. When I left town to be with Ken during his last days in his earthly body, many people asked me to deliver a message of friendship and appreciation to him and his beautiful wife, Gaea, which I did. I heard things like, "Tell Ken whenever I turn on my air-conditioner, I think of him and thank him for installing it for me." "Tell Ken how much I appreciated his help when I moved." "Tell Ken how important he was to my recovery from addiction and how he helped me feel comfortable in a church again."

I look around my own home and office, and I see Ken everywhere. He installed the shelves in my office for my antique radio collection. He came to my rescue many times, such as when I attempted to install a huge retractable awning over my patio. I finally swallowed my male pride and called Ken. Then I awkwardly stood by, trying to look like I knew which drill bit or wrench or some other tool he had just asked for that I had never heard of. He never made me feel inadequate. I did that all by myself.

It seems cliché to say that friendship is too precious to take for granted, but it is. Take an opportunity to extend yourself to your friends, especially the ones you have let slip away for one reason or another. Make a phone call, write a letter, or send an email just because they matter and it matters to you to let them know how important they are to you. For extra credit, take the risk and extend yourself to someone who is not yet a friend. We all need friends and friendly encounters with others. Your simple gesture of friendship can make a huge difference in someone's life. Take notice of folks, see into them, offer a welcoming presence, a friendly face and smile, and be the one to reach out in friendship. Every little act of friendship contributes to a larger energy force that helps create a world where no one is excluded.

2007

"The most I can do for my friend is simply to be his friend. I have no wealth to bestow on him. If he knows I am happy in loving him he will want no other reward. Is not friendship divine in this?"

Henry David Thoreau

Keeping a Divine Appointment

"Open your eyes; look within. Are you satisfied with the life you are living?"
Bob Marley

One of the most enriching aspects of being a minister is conducting memorial services for families. In some rare instances, I have the opportunity to meet with the person facing imminent death to discuss his or her beliefs about life, death, purpose, and his or her desires for the memorial service, which I call the Celebration of Life. What a privilege it is to discuss end-of-life issues with a person and his or her family. It is healthy to approach the end of this life expression openly and honestly. Often, there is great reluctance on the part of family members to release their loved one, and they shut off any attempts to broach the subject. That saddens me because in most situations the dying person wants, and needs, to talk it through.

Years ago I did my chaplain residency at Baptist Hospital in Kansas City, Kansas. When I arrived for my shift, I was given the list of patients who had been assigned to me. I was to visit each one and minister to them as best I could. That afternoon I was tired and out of sorts. I didn't want to minister to anyone that night. I felt in need of a chaplain myself, but there I was. One of the names on my list was a woman who had just had major surgery and experienced serious complications. She had requested a visit. I walked into her room, saw that she was sleeping peacefully, and selfishly thought to myself, *oh, good, I'll just leave my card, a note, and a Daily Word.* I stood by her bed and said a prayer for her and her medical team. I was filling out my report before I left her room, when I became aware of the woman in the bed by the door. She was surrounded by her children, who were waiting for her to be released that afternoon. She sat quietly in her bed while her children bustled around her, fluffing pillows, pouring water, and talking animatedly about trivial matters. I walked past her bed on the way out but felt a nudge to stop and speak to her. I stood at the end of her hospital bed and our eyes met. She had soft, kind, sad eyes.

I joked with her and commented, "Well, you look like you are being well taken care of. You have trained them well." Her kids seemed very nervous and kept reassuring her that she was fine and soon would be her old self again. The woman ignored them and kept her eyes locked on mine. Then she said, "I am checking out soon." The kids continued to chatter. I instinctively knew she wasn't referring to checking out of the hospital; she was soon to check out of this life. I said, "You seem to have great peace with that." She replied, "I do have peace. I have had a wonderful life, and it is my time." The nervous energy among her children amped up noticeably, and they admonished her, "Oh, Mom, stop that! You're going to be fine. You'll outlive us all."

She ignored them and continued looking at me. I asked her what was so wonderful about her life, and she went on to tell me about her late husband, who she would be joining soon, her children and grandchildren, the travels they had enjoyed with the family, and so on. I just listened, fully aware this was the only way she could communicate to her children that she was dying soon and wanted them to know she was at peace. I remember thinking, *Ah, this is why I am here. I was sent to this room not for the sleeping woman in the other bed, but to be with this dying woman so she could use me to communicate her truth, which her children had been stifling.* The room was quiet now, and one of her daughters, starting to cry, bent down to hug her mother. One of her sons glared at me. I knew my work was complete now, and I wished her a safe journey and a glorious reunion with her husband. She looked at me with gratitude as I left. We smiled a secret, knowing smile and nodded. I walked out feeling lighter and grateful that Spirit had used in me in this way. In Unity, we often refer to our Divine Appointments, and I felt this was definitely one of those.

We all have a Divine Appointment with death (yes, you, too), and the best way to prepare is to start discussing your wishes and beliefs with family and friends sooner, not later. If you are open and unembarrassed about death, your family and friends will likely take their cues from you. The conspiracy of silence many people enter into concerning death robs everyone of the rich gifts of authenticity, reconciliation, and closure. If you have not yet prepared an advanced health care directive, please take the important action to do so. It is one of the kindest things you can do to assist your family and friends cope with your passing when that time comes. It is also a great way to start the conversation with them about what you want. By the way, this is easier to do when you are well.

In the meantime, live as you will want to have lived when you are dying. Carpe diem!

February 2012

"Your living is determined not so much by what life brings to you as by the attitude you bring to life; not so much by what happens to you but by the way your mind looks at what happens."

Khalil Gibran

Letting Go of What's Not Working

"Some of us think holding on makes us strong; but sometimes it is letting go."

Hermann Hesse

As a child growing up in the Catholic Church, I didn't find Lent, the forty-day period before Easter, a very uplifting time. It was a very solemn time when all the statues and icons were draped in purple, and even the joyous sounds of the mass bells were silenced. I especially did not like that because I was the altar boy who enthusiastically rang the bells during mass. That was my moment to shine.

Lent was also a time when we were expected to fast from, or give up as a sacrifice, something we enjoyed. I didn't like that sacrifice thing a bit. I did not like to hear the word "no" from anyone, especially myself. Truthfully, that youth still lives in me today, although a bit tamer now...but not much.

As I have matured, I now view Lent and fasting in a more positive light. Every legitimate spiritual path asks its followers to set aside specific periods during the year for fasting and

self-examination. It is a time to reestablish control over the immature and unenlightened aspects of ourselves that still want to rule
the roost without concern for the good of the rest of the house-
hold. Lent offers us a time to exercise spiritual adulthood.

Today I see great spiritual value in establishing discipline over
my less than healthy thoughts, attitudes, and appetites. I have never regretted the times I set aside for sober reflection, courageous
self-examination, and spiritual redirection. Lent is one of those
special times during each year when we can choose to reset our
inner guidance systems by letting go of (or dying to) those old
attitudes and habits that do not serve our higher natures.

Faith and I used to jokingly refer to the immature aspect of
our beings as the "*little twit within*." We all have one, and it always
wants its own way and throws temper tantrums when it is denied.
Our *little twit within* lives in a world of self-righteousness, self-consciousness, and self-centeredness. The truth is the *little twit within*
has only as much power as we allow it. Our true power is our divine
self, or the Christ within. This is what we are called to be, but first
we must let go of everything unlike it and move toward living a life
that serves the highest and best in ourselves and our world.

I invite you to consciously participate in Lent, or a period of
fasting, by taking time to reflect on what is not working in your
life and be willing to take some *authentic action* to eliminate it and
replace it with something life-affirming. We can start by using the
acronym L.E.N.T.: Let's Eliminate Negative Thinking!

While that is an excellent place to start, I suggest we take it much deeper. As we fast from negative thoughts, attitudes, and habits, let us also feast on the positive by adding a spiritually uplifting activity to our daily lives, such as keeping a gratitude journal in which we list five things for which we are grateful each day. Lent is a perfect time to begin or restart an exercise program or renew our New Year's intentions if they have fallen away. You know what you must do.

It takes just forty days to develop a new habit. Make this forty-day period count for something positive and life-changing; otherwise, when Easter arrives, nothing will have changed. You will still be a prisoner of your past with the *little twit within* as your jailer. Easter is about renewal, redemption, and resurrection. Lent is a forty-day period to help us create that new life.

February 2008

"The very nature of kindness is to spread. If you are kind to others, today they will be kind to you, and tomorrow to somebody else. Be kind always."

Sri Chinmoy

Violence to One's Soul

"I spawn suspicion and generate grief. I cause many sleepless nights and make innocent people weep into their pillows. Even my name hisses. I am Gossip."

Author unknown

"Psst! Have you heard the latest?"

Recently the Harris Poll surveyed fifteen hundred office workers and asked what their number-one pet peeve was concerning the work environment. How would you answer that question? Perhaps messiness, loud noises, misuse of email, or poor time-management skills of others? All of those were mentioned, but the number-one pet peeve was gossip. Almost two-thirds of those surveyed said gossip was pervasive and toxic.

Human beings are social animals—we love to talk, tell stories, and share information. It is what makes us unique in the animal kingdom. Most of the information shared between two people about another is of the innocent, neutral kind—a romance, a promotion, and so on. But when does normal or necessary communication become gossip? I think the answer is when the information is of a negative nature, and it is spread with a malicious intent to harm another's standing or reputation.

We have all participated in some form of gossip or another. It is hard not to since it is so pervasive in our society. We also seem to be hard-wired for it since the Stone Age. I have done it, I have passively let it happen, and I have spread it on. Look at the nature of our political campaign system—it seems to depend on the spreading of malicious information and rumors, true or not, about opponents or anyone even connected to them.

There are times when it may be necessary to share uncomfortable information about another for the good of the whole, but the difference is that the intention is not to harm or diminish that person in the process. John Lavater, a sixteenth-century poet, cautioned, "Never tell evil of another if you do not know it for a certainty, and even if you know for a certainty, ask yourself 'Why should I tell this?' It's the underlying intention that matters."

A few years ago, I was studying the nonviolent practices of Mahatma Gandhi and Dr. Martin Luther King, Jr. and found gossip described as one of the most insidious forms of violence. I had never thought of it in those terms, but it made perfect sense. While physical violence is unthinkable to most of us, we do not think of gossip as a violent act, but, in truth, gossip is violence to another's soul. It maims without killing. It has ended careers and lifelong friendships, broken up families, caused divorces, destroyed reputations and self-esteem, toppled governments, and even led to extreme physical violence such as murder and suicide. Think about it—gossip is dense, dark, destructive energy. It has no life-affirming value. It is nobody's friend.

It was then I decided to refrain from gossiping or listening to it and to launch my own private campaign to form gossip-free zones. I invite you to join me in this spiritual practice of nonviolence by creating gossip-free zones in your homes, classrooms, and places of work.

Gossipmongers often start their slam sessions with something like, "Now, you know I'm not one to stir the pot," or "I'm not one to gossip," or "You didn't hear it from me, okay?" There are also more so-called "spiritual" and subtle ways to spread the crud, such as, "Mary needs our prayers; I hear she and Bob are having marriage troubles...again. He may be drinking heavily...again." It may seem innocent and even high-minded, but it is still spreading unverified information that can only do harm.

Here are some practical ways to deal with gossip and gossipmongers.

- Don't participate. Walk away or change the subject. Show no interest.
- Speak up. "I'm not comfortable talking about someone else behind his/her back because I don't appreciate it when someone else does it to me."
- Stop them and say, "Wait, I hadn't heard that. Let's go ask him/her if it's true." This usually causes the "deer in the headlights" look on the gossipmonger's face.

- If you are the subject of gossip, go directly to the person and say, "I heard you are saying the following about me. I would appreciate it if you would stop now. In the future, if you want to know something, please come to me directly to check the facts before talking with others."
- Don't be a gossipmonger yourself. Gossip says more about the gossipmonger than the one being maligned. Remember, what goes around comes around. Gossipmongers do great damage to their own souls and sense of self-worth. No one trusts or respects them. No one.
- Remember, not everything shared about another is gossip; it is only those words intended to do harm or demean another's standing or reputation. Before sharing possibly harmful information about another, ask yourself these three questions:

> Is it true?
>
> Is it kind?
>
> Is it necessary?

"IF...it's very painful to criticize your friends, then you are safe in doing it. But if you take even the slightest pleasure, that's the time to hold your tongue."

Alice Duer Miller

Trusting Your Intuition

"I often feel there are two people inside me—me and my intuition. If I go against her, she'll screw me every time, but if I listen to and follow her, we get along quite nicely."

Kim Bassinger

My morning started out so well. I slept like a well-fed baby, woke up refreshed, jumped out of bed, and arrived at the levee parking lot before 5:00 a.m. As I waited for my walking partners, I turned up the volume on my Van Morrison CD. He was singing one of my favorite feel-good songs, "There'll Be Days Like This." There I was in a lonely, dark, foggy parking lot singing unselfconsciously in my best Van Morrison voice these positive, uplifting lyrics:

"When it's not always rainin', there'll be days like this.
When there's no one complainin', there'll be days like this.
Everything falls into place like the flick of a switch,
Well, my momma told me there'll be days like this.

When you don't need to worry, there'll be days like this.
When no one's in a hurry, there'll be days like this.

When you don't get betrayed by that ole' Judas kiss,
Well, my momma told me there'll be days like this."

Oh, I was feeling it. This was one of those days Momma promised me!

My partners arrived, and we began our ritual walk on a very damp, foggy, almost eerie morning. As we left the parking lot, something made me turn back to look at my car. I felt a little uneasy, so I clicked the remote lock one more time to be sure.

I was in high spirits as we walked and talked, and then I got the "hit." The "hit" was an impression that my car was being broken into. I ignored it; after all, we had parked our cars in exactly the same spot several days a week for many years, and nothing had ever happened. I walked on, talking animatedly about the author and speaker I had heard the night before at the Mondavi Center in Davis. Then I got the "hit" one more time. I shook it off, thinking it was just the fog that was spooking me. *Don't be silly*, I thought, *no one is messing with your car.*

You have probably guessed by now that my car was indeed broken into and emptied of its contents, including my Van Morrison CDs. To add insult to injury, mine was the only car broken into. Hmm, Momma hadn't mentioned "there'll be days like this!"

What was interesting to me was when I first saw the shattered glass, I wasn't even surprised because I had already "seen" it at least three times during the walk but had brushed it off as an overly active imagination fueled by the eerie fog along the dark levee.

My annoyance at the destructive thief was almost immediately replaced by annoyance at myself for dismissing clear intuitive guidance from my Higher Self. My angels were probably saying, "Man, sometimes he can be so dense. What does it take with this guy? I mean, come on, three times we told him! Why didn't he listen?"

"Why didn't I listen?" That is the question I asked myself many times during that day. The answer is I didn't really trust my inner guidance, even though it has never once let me down. My ego-self was unwilling to interrupt our morning routine on just a "hunch." I didn't want to appear foolish or "woo-woo." Boy, do I feel foolish now. My self-consciousness and doubt cost me hundreds of dollars and a great deal of inconvenience. Woo!

Perhaps my expensive lesson will remind you to be more mindful when your sixth sense, or intuitive self, attempts to guide and protect you. That is its only function. It is the "still small voice" of scripture.

We all have intuition. The more we pay attention to it and practice using it, the more adept we become at recognizing its voice above all the other voices of self-judgment, doubt, self-consciousness, and fear. It can and will keep us out of many embarrassing, dangerous, and expensive mistakes. Trust me on this one.

The great Albert Einstein said, "The intuitive mind is a sacred gift and the rational mind is a faithful servant. We have created a society that honors the servant but has forgotten the gift. The only real valuable thing is intuition." Amen to that.

March 2009

"You have to leave the city of your comfort and go into the wilderness of your intuition. What you will discover will be wonderful; you will discover your true wonderful self."

Alan Alda

Family, The Cutting Edge of Relationships
Is There An "Aunt Francis" in Your Life?

"We all grow up with the weight of history on us. Our ancestors dwell in the attics of our brains as they do in the spiraling chains of knowledge hidden in every cell of our bodies."

Shirley Abbott

While slowly going through decades of letters, cards, and memorabilia from my life, I discovered an eloquent letter written by my Aunt Francis, who was also my godmother. My sister, Patti, and I were her favorite niece and nephew, and my father was her favorite brother—at least that's how Patti and I remember it. Francis and I even resembled one another, and people often mistook her for my mother.

I loved Aunt Francis but also feared her and never quite felt accepted by her. I remembered her as a critical, stern, Irish schoolteacher and high school principal whom I could never please. Since she was matriarch of the Moran clan, her opinion carried a lot of weight. She was both feared and revered. When my daughter was born, we named her Jennifer Francis Moran in her honor.

During my early thirties as I was going through a difficult time dealing with the death of my mother, my divorce, and a career upheaval, plus the beginnings of a major spiritual awakening, I found myself disconnected from my aunt. For some long-forgotten reason, I had distanced myself from her over something she must have said or I thought she said. I totally cut her out of my life, probably because I felt judged. She was a staunch Irish Catholic, and divorce was not tolerated. I remember feeling like the failure of the family as I was the first Moran to divorce and to leave the Church.

While sitting on a box in the middle of my cluttered garage, I found an old tattered valise containing letters from that period of time. In it, I found a letter in which Aunt Francis sincerely apologized for whatever she had said or done that angered me and caused me to shut her out. She was obviously baffled by my extreme reaction and affirmed her love for me and her desire to make it right. She even told me she knew how difficult it must be for me to grieve the loss of my mom and then go through a divorce at the same time. I could read the hurt and confusion in her words almost thirty years later. She repeatedly affirmed her love and support for me. That day, I had no recollection of ever having received or read this beautiful letter, but, fortunately for some reason, I kept it.

As I reread the letter, I tried to remember what was so awful that I would turn my back on someone who had loved me all my life. Try as I might, I could not recollect a reason. What a shame. Aunt Francis was not the softest, most cuddly person in the world, but she was the product of a very different era and culture. Along with my Aunt Marion, she helped raise her three younger brothers and our cousins, the four Sullivan boys, after their parents were killed. Francis and Marion never married; instead, they devoted their lives to the care and well-being of the two families while living in a small walk-up on Chicago's south side.

As I read her beautiful letter, my mind flooded with memories of all the wonderful, fun times I enjoyed with her and the opportunities and adventures she provided my sister, mother, and me after my dad died. It felt great to remember the goodness of her heart instead of her awkward verbal communication skills when it came to expressing her love, fears, and concerns. Aunt Francis has been gone almost thirty years now, and she died not knowing why our relationship ended so abruptly. I don't even remember why. How sad.

I wonder: how many times do we shut someone out of our lives over a trivial comment or even a major faux pas that we stubbornly refuse to let go? I have a feeling it is more often than most of us would care to admit. The good news is that it is never too late to set it right. I believe prayer is the language of Spirit, and that no soul, living or dead, present or far away, is ever beyond the reach and power of loving thoughts and sacred intentions.

How could I make it right? Here's what I did. I took a moment to center myself and brought my Aunt Francis to mind. I connected with her heart. Once I felt her, I talked to her from my soul to her soul. I asked for her forgiveness for my immature actions of long ago. I told her how much I appreciated all she had done for me and my family as we struggled after Dad's death. I acknowledged my thoughtlessness and immaturity and apologized for any pain I caused her. I told her I loved her. I surrounded her with loving energy and good thoughts. Then the more mature person I have become today forgave that young, hurt, immature person I was at that time.

Did any of this matter in the grand cosmic sense? Who knows? It mattered to me, and I hope it mattered to her. The whole experience reminded me to give people the benefit of the doubt and a second chance, and to reopen my heart to those I have harshly judged or by whom I felt unfairly judged. I made the promise to Aunt Francis and to myself that my current stories of her would be the positive, life-affirming ones that truly comprised 95 percent of our lives together instead of retelling a few old, hurtful stories that put her in a negative light.

Any time is a good time for courageous self-reflection, humble acknowledgment of poor choices, and sincere attempts at reconciliation. I invite you to consider releasing grudges and ego-driven pettiness. Take time to reconnect via phone, snail mail, email, or prayer mail with those living or dead who have helped grow and shape you into the beautiful person emerging as you today.

Thank you, Aunt Francis, for your beautiful, heartfelt letter. It arrived just in time. It reminded me I still have work to do.

February 2008

"You can give without loving, but you cannot love without giving."

Robert Louis Stevenson

Our Furry Friends

"All of the animals except man know that the principle business of life is to enjoy it."

Samuel Butler

My friend Jim's dog was dying, and he was deeply grieving the loss of his loyal friend and companion, Max. This lovable dog proved to be the one constant in my friend's life for thirteen years when he faced many challenges. No matter what, Max never wavered in his loyalty or love.

The death of loved ones is always devastating as we struggle to come to terms with life without their physical presence. Often, when it is a beloved pet that has passed, people will say, "I know it must seem silly for me to grieve so deeply because it is only my pet." I always reassure them that, on the contrary, our pets come to us as great teachers of unconditional love, and they become treasured members of our families. Sometimes they are the most loyal friends we have ever known.

Often the loss of pets is even more difficult because they offer us unwavering love without agendas. We love them, talk to them, hug and kiss them. Our pets don't judge us when we neglect them or hold grudges. They overlook our shortcomings and forgive quickly when we scold them. A beloved pet could care less if the house is clean or if we are having a bad hair day. They just love us and shower us with affection and acceptance with no conditions. There is nothing like coming home to a pet that greets you like you are the most important person in the world and your homecoming is the absolute high point of his or her day. No wonder we love our pets so.

Our pets teach us responsibility by their total dependence upon us for care and feeding. Anyone who has ever lost a pet due to some temporary neglect or accident often experiences intense pain and has difficulty forgiving themselves for years. And yet it is such a gift to be the guardian of an animal who thinks you are the best human on earth.

I have helped five of my beloved dogs, Tippy, Harmony, Miss Scarlet, Goldie the Wonder Dog, and Bridget, make the transition from life to death when their suffering became too great, or hopefully just before that time. In each case it was one of the most gutwrenching and loving decisions I have ever made. It is not something anyone takes lightly.

Our pets make it easy for us to be exuberant and playful with our show of love and affection. They just let us love them, soak it up, and send it right back. They really understand and practice the Law of Karma, "What goes around comes around." What would happen if we treated everyone in our lives with as much acceptance, kindness, patience, and love as we show our "fur angels"?

Better yet, what if we treated everyone in our lives the way our pets treat us?

Good dog, Max! God speed old friend.

"The purity of a person's heart can be measured by the way they regard animals."

Unknown

Parents as People

"Seeking to forget makes exile even longer; the secret to redemption is in remembrance."
Richard von Weizaecker

Jo, a church member and friend, shared a touching story about her relationship with her father, Bill. When Jo was growing up, her dad was a blue-collar worker and president of his union at the local paper mill in a grimy, smelly, little Minnesota town she referred to as "the outskirts of hell." She said her dad was kind, quiet, boring, and for many years an alcoholic who was too often in the hospital for his "nervous condition."

Like many teenagers, Jo suffered from low self-esteem. She constantly compared her family and herself to others and felt her life would be happy if only...if only...if only. Jo described her teen self as "ugly, fat, frizzled, and goggled." She went on to say, "I was also Catholic. Oh, what a ripe setting for low self-esteem. I did not disappoint the low-self-esteem God. I paid my homage daily. I was depressed, homely, and desperately wanted to get away and start somewhere fresh where no one knew me or where I had come from. I graduated high school and left for California three days later! I began a new life and never looked back on that hick town, which had bored me to tears and left me feeling inadequate and homely." (Knowing Jo today, it is hard to imagine her old self-image.)

Many years later, Jo, her sister, and her dad, now retired, sober, and living in Sacramento, returned to visit the "outskirts of hell," where they experienced a great surprise. The town had totally transformed itself, and civic pride was evident everywhere. The smelly, dirty paper mill where her father labored was as clean and fresh as a bakery. The former classmates to whom she had unfavorably compared herself had helped reinvent the "outskirts of hell" into a delightful town.

The biggest "ah-ha" came when Jo observed how her dad was received by his fellow workers, who now referred to him as the smartest union president ever since those early years. His negotiation skills were unsurpassed, and the union workers were still benefiting twenty years later from his professionalism and loyalty to them.

Jo's eyes and heart were opened when she learned that her alcoholic father had given up drinking because he found out the mill management considered him to be an easily manipulated drunk. The young man who was going to run for vice president of the union alongside Bill had visited him in the hospital, where he was drying out one more time. He told Bill he was not going to run with him because management considered Bill to be a "laughing-stock and that they would make asses out of the both of them." Jo's dad promised that young man he would stop drinking for good and not let him or the union down. If they didn't run, Bill said, the union would suffer, and many benefits would be lost. They ran together and won.

From that time on, Jo's dad kept his word and remained sober. A family mystery was now solved. Jo said, "Our whole family never knew what made Dad stop drinking, but we knew something powerful had happened in the hospital that last time."

She continued, "The businesses that were run by the fathers of the girls I envied in high school were all gone now, but the mill where my father gave many years of loyalty and leadership was not only still there but better than ever. I know in my heart that a substantial part of that success was due to him. I smile remembering how the people at the mill said to my sister and me as they reached out to us, 'Oh, you're Bill Bernicke's daughter. What a pleasure to meet you. He was the best ever!'

"What a pleasure to be his daughter, I thought, bursting with pride. My dad was *really somebody* in town and was still remembered fondly twenty years later. I felt so honored and so proud of him."

As the saying goes, "We come full circle when we stand in the place we started and see it again for the first time." Jo's journey home completed a full circle, and what she found was new appreciation for her hometown, her father, and herself.

June 2007

"Every father should remember that one day his child will follow his example rather than his advice."

Unknown

Honoring Our Mothers

"Mother is the name of God in the lips and hearts of little children."
William Makepeace Thackery

Every May we celebrate Mother's Day in the United States. It is always bittersweet for me as I reflect on my own mother, who died in 1977 at the young age of sixty-two. My mother was, by far, the most influential person in my life. She not only gave me life, she modeled how genuinely good and honorable people conduct themselves throughout life. My mother was far from perfect, but she was the perfect mom for me. She offered me exactly the right blend of toughness and gentleness. I am especially grateful for her toughness during my testosterone-driven teenage years when I was self-centered and rebellious. I tested her mightily after the death of my father when I was twelve, but she dug in her heels and held me 100 percent accountable for my self-destructive behavior. My mom rarely cut me slack, but I always knew beyond a doubt that she loved me unconditionally, even when she asked a juvenile court judge to give me the maximum punishment allowable for a minor first infraction.

Mother's Day in the United States is observed each year on the second Sunday in May. It is a day to honor mothers and those who have acted as mother figures in our lives. Few people remember that it is also a day to promote peace. In 1870, Unitarian abolitionist Julia Ward Howe, who wrote the "Battle Hymn of the Republic," also proposed that Mothers' Peace Day should be a call for peace and disarmament. The United States had just been through the Civil War, its bloodiest conflict, which caused more than a million casualties and claimed 620,000 lives. The nation was still deeply divided and wounded.

Julia Ward Howe felt that only women were motivated enough to bring an end to the insanity of men raining hell on each other as a means to settle conflict. In 1870, she wrote the Mother's Day Peace Proclamation. Here is a portion of it:

"Arise then…women of this day! Arise all women who have hearts!

Whether your baptism be of water or of tears!

Say firmly:

We will not have questions answered by irrelevant agencies.

Our husbands will not come to us, reeking with carnage for caresses and applause.

Our sons shall not be taken from us to unlearn all that we have been able to teach them of charity, mercy, and patience.

We, the women of one country, will be too tender of those of another country, to allow our sons to be trained to injure theirs."

In addition to more emphasis on peace, I wish there were less hype about traditional motherhood and more acknowledgment of not-so-traditional "mothers" in our midst—people who come in all colors, shapes, sizes genders, and ages. And, more than anything, I wish there were a lot more empathy for those who suffer from not being acknowledged on Mother's Day. Katie Lee Crane says it well:

"Sadly, I don't trust Hallmark to remember the feelings of the women who don't fit Mother's Day in quite the same wonderful way. There are no cards on the rack for women who gave up children for adoption, never to see them again. No cards for women who faced the painful and difficult choice to end a pregnancy. No cards for women who desperately want to conceive and bear children and cannot. No cards for women who have lost children of any age or for the women whose children have abandoned them in anger. There is little consolation for them on a day so full of 'motherhood and apple pie.'"

Let us honor them all on Mother's Day—women who conceived, women who bore, women who reared, women who lost, women who let go, women who made different choices, and people of any gender who mother and nurture others.

This year, and in the future, in addition to giving the "moms in your life" the gifts of cards, flowers, and a well-deserved meal cooked by someone else, give her the gift of *peace*. Offer a prayer for the end of war, terrorism, and domestic violence. Be a dreamer, and imagine a future when no mother has to mourn the death of a child or a loved one because of the insanity of terrorism and war.

To all mothers who are fighting in wars, or whose children are fighting, or who are innocently caught in the crossfire, may you experience peace, courage, and hope for a peaceful world.

May 2010

"The moment a child is born, a mother is also born. She never existed until that moment. The woman existed, but the mother, never. A mother is something absolutely new."

Unknown

Honoring Our Fathers

"It doesn't matter who my father was; it matters who I remember he was."

Anne Sexton

Every year in May we celebrate Mother's Day and, in June, Father's Day to honor mothers and dads and those people, male and female, who served as parental figures in our lives. As a minister, I have found it interesting to observe how differently the vast majority of people approach these traditions. Mother's Day always gets much more interest and involvement from the many congregations I have served over the decades. I checked with some of my minister friends, and they reported the same thing: Mother's Day is observed with much more enthusiasm and depth of emotion, while Father's Day is celebrated but not with the same level of interest.

On Mother's Day, attendance tends to go up as mothers sometimes drag along reluctant husbands and children who normally don't share their interest in spirituality. On Father's Day, attendance often goes down as dads take a day off to do what they want with little or no resistance. Once again, it seems to support an old generalization that women are more social and want family and friends around them at special times, whereas men, who tend to be more solitary, don't. No judgment here, just an observation.

A study done by a think-tank organization called Australian Institute came to some conclusions that were not all that surprising. In short, women were far more likely than their male counterparts to feel "connected" by friendships and other social ties. A far greater number of women agreed with the statements, "I seem to have a lot of friends" or "There is always someone I can count on to cheer me up when I am down or lonely." Across all age groups, the majority of men agreed with the statements, "People don't call or visit me often" or "There is no one I can/will confide in."

Having been a "lone wolf" for much of my life, I have found that life is much richer when I take the risk to reach out and let others in, especially men. I had to force myself to learn this because, like many men I know, I learned not to trust other men. As we grew out of childhood, we were taught in subtle and obvious ways to compete with and dominate other men for touchdowns, knockouts, women, jobs, or success. It is the old "law of the jungle," which works great in the jungle but really limits our enjoyment of friendships with men in our lives.

I must say I have recently witnessed a refreshing change in the old "solitary man" paradigm. I watch young dads today who are much more involved in the raising and care-giving of their children. It warms my heart and gives me hope. My sons and son-in-law are much more intimately involved in the care and nurturing of their children than my father's and my generations.

Kirk D. Loadman-Copeland of the Unitarian Universalist Church wrote "A Fathers' Day Prayer."

"Let us praise those fathers who have striven to balance the demand of work, marriage and children with an honest awareness of both joy and sacrifice. Let us praise those fathers who, lacking a good model for a father, have worked to become a good father.

"Let us praise those fathers who by their own account were not always there for their children, but who continue to offer those children, now grown, their love and support. Let us pray for those fathers who have been wounded by the neglect and hostility of their children.

"Let us praise those fathers who, despite divorce, have remained in their children's lives. Let us praise those fathers whose children are adopted, and whose love and support has offered healing.

"Let us praise those fathers who, as stepfathers, freely choose the obligation of fatherhood and earned their stepchildren's love and respect. Let us praise those fathers who have lost a child to death, and continue to hold the child in their heart.

"Let us praise those men who have no children, but cherish the next generation as if they were their own. Let us praise those men who have 'fathered' us in their role as mentors and guides.

"Let us praise those men who are about to become fathers; may they openly delight in their children. And let us praise those fathers who have died, but live on in our memory and whose love continues to nurture us."

June 2009

"To forgive is the highest, most beautiful form of love; in return you will receive untold peace and happiness."

Dr. Robert Muller

Best End of the Deal

"Love is eternal; the aspect may change but not the true essence."

Vincent Van Gogh

On anniversary days of our lives, we tend to reflect on the years preceding and the events that led us to that Divine Appointment. It's important to do so—it gives us a sense of perspective and continuity.

July 9, 2008, would have been Faith's and my twenty-fifth wedding anniversary and, as the first anniversary since her death, represented another "new normal" for me. Each anniversary, Faith and I would follow the same ritual. No matter where in the world we happened to be, we would open the special box we normally kept on our home altar. It contained our vows, candles, a cassette tape of the ceremony, and some wedding pictures. On the lid of the box Faith had inscribed, "Today I marry my best friend." We would light the candle and once again speak our personal vows to each other as we exchanged our Irish (Claddaugh) wedding rings.

This ritual reminded us of the intense level of love and commitment we promised each other at the beginning of our journey together as husband and wife. We had both been married before, and we were determined to do it differently this time. We were fully aware of how difficult it is to not just say the vows but to pray them and live them.

Next, we would share a glass of mighty fine wine from the wedding chalice we bought for that special day, July 9, 1983, and toast each other with the Irish Claddaugh blessing, "May love, friendship, and loyalty reign above all else in our lives." Afterward, we would reminisce and speak our intentions for our next year together as best friends and husband and wife.

During some really tough years of studying, working together, ministering, and parenting, we struggled at times to stay connected. Life tests us in ways that we cannot foresee. Those vows and the annual reenactment of our ceremony served as powerful reminders of the promises we made to be there for each other "no matter what." We also hung a small framed calligraphy piece on our bedroom wall that stated *Love Is a Decision*. That little reminder helped us decide to stay in love during those painful, awkward, "out of sync" times every genuine relationship goes through. I never once questioned my deep love for Faith, but there were times, for both of us, when we had to decide to **be loving** toward one another... even when, or especially when, frustrated, disillusioned, exhausted by life's challenges, or just feeling distant.

At one point after about eight years of marriage, we both grew restless and dissatisfied. At first we thought something was wrong, but two wise teachers, Foster and Paula McClellan, a couple we both admired, told us that we were being asked to go deeper and discover a whole new dimension of love, passion, and purpose. We worked through it and recommitted to our lives together and to each other at a whole new and more mature level. These same wise mentors taught us, "The key to a lasting marriage is when both parties treat each other as if they got the best end of the deal." (This is profound and works wonders!)

I feel good about our marriage and friendship. It is something I think we both could point to and say, "We got it right this time." Even knowing how it would end and what would be required of us, I would sign on again and again and again with no hesitation. Some things are worth any price asked.

The attitude of acting as if we each got the best part of the deal allows us to come from a position of gratitude and a positive outlook. So, ask yourself about your important relationships:

- Is my life better today because of my involvement with and support of this relationship?
- Has this friendship made a positive and tangible difference in my life?
- Am I making a genuine effort to keep this relationship alive, vital, and authentic?
- Am I willing to step up and recommit to this relationship so I can take myself and it to an even deeper level of spiritual maturity and service through my physical presence and commitment?
- Am I willing to act as if I got the best part of the deal?

July 2008

"Some people come into our lives and quickly leave. Some stay for a while and leave footprints on our hearts. And we are never, ever the same."

Unknown

Facing Adversity
Moving On

"There are times when two people need to step apart from one another, but there is no rule that says they have to turn and fire."

Robert Brault

One of the most painful and perplexing life situations is when a close personal relationship changes for no apparent reason and suddenly someone you considered a friend for life is no longer. That person, who occupied a very special place in your heart reserved for a precious few, has suddenly removed him- or herself, and you are clueless as to the reason why. You feel confounded, hurt, angry, sad, and sometimes guilty, wondering what you did to cause such a drastic and permanent rift. Many times the cause is obvious, such as a betrayal of some sort, and it still hurts, but you have a reason and with time you can eventually reconcile it. Sometimes life circumstances take someone away, never to be seen again, and we evolve in different directions. It is sad, but that is just life.

A while ago, a man (let's call him Bob) came to me heart-sick over the loss of a close friendship since early childhood. He and his friend grew up in the same neighborhood, rode their bikes to school every day, served as scouts, went through puberty learning about women by sneaking peeks at the lingerie section in the Sears catalogue, played sports, and were the best man in each other's weddings. They were best friends, closer than brothers. Even when they moved to separate parts of the country, they stayed in regular contact and, in most years, met for fishing and skiing excursions. Then one day out of the blue, Bob's lifelong buddy dropped out, saying he no longer felt a connection. He wanted no further contact. He had moved on. That was it. Bob pressed his friend for a reason, and his friend went on to tell him how many ways Bob had let him down over the years. Bob was stunned since he didn't recall any of the incidents mentioned, at least not the way they were presented.

As I listened to Bob's story, I tried to stay focused on him, but memories came flooding back to me of people who had played key roles in my life who were no longer there. Some I knew why or suspected the reasons they had split, and still others were complete mysteries. I also thought of times when it was reversed, and I was the one who no longer felt a close bond, and it was I who ended a relationship "just because." That specialness you once felt for the other gradually dissolved and you can't put your finger on when or why. I think we have all been on both sides of this, and it is never a pleasant experience for either party. The ambiguity can be maddening, especially for the one being left behind.

So what is it all about? I could ponder on this endlessly, but I think it boils down to everyone and everything in life serving a purpose. Once that purpose has been fulfilled, or it becomes obvious on some level it will never be fulfilled in that relationship, we gradually disconnect emotionally, and this is followed, sooner or later, by a physical separation. Lives change, priorities shift, shared perspectives are no longer. We become different people, grow apart spiritually, politically, and so forth, and one day we look at our "lifelong" friend and realize we don't have anything in common anymore. It has happened to all of us, and most likely it will happen again. That is the nature of life; people and things always change. People come and people go, meeting certain needs or offering us our life lessons, and then move on.

The sad thing is that too often, instead of acknowledging we are now different people and are moving on, we project failure onto the other person, make them wrong, and create some drama to justify our decision. It is an all-too-familiar scenario. I think that's what happened to Bob. Unfortunately, his old best friend spewed vitriol and made it all about Bob, when it was quite likely the other way around. I gave Bob my copy of Don Miguel Ruiz's book *The Four Agreements* to give him some insight as he heals from this loss. The second agreement is, "Nothing other people do is because of you; it is because of them. Don't take anything personally." I know it is easier said than done, but it is true. Of course, we still have to honestly examine our role in every relationship and own what is ours.

By the time he came to see me, Bob had been in pain for some time and was seeking release. He said something I have heard myself say, "I never dreamed of the day this person wouldn't be a major part of my life." I asked, "Assuming your former friend's decision is irrevocable, how would you like this to be different?" He thought for some time and then said, "I would like to be able to fully accept it, quit obsessing about what went wrong, remember the good times without feeling such sadness and loss, and feel happiness and peace again. I want to move on."

Ah, now we were getting somewhere. Bob identified what he wanted to bring into his life instead of focusing only on what was missing. I asked, "What can you do starting now that will help bring that about?" After an extended time of silence, Bob blessed his former friend, forgave him for the immature and unskilled way he ended the friendship, and chose to cherish the love and memories they had created during their many years of friendship. It was a great start. This process will probably have to be repeated often until the full healing takes place. In the army I learned: "Stop the bleeding. Clean wound thoroughly. Change bandages. Repeat as often as necessary." The same directions apply for emotional and spiritual wounds as well.

Shakespeare said it best in *As You Like It*: "All the world's a stage, and all the men and women merely players; they have their exits and entrances; and one man plays many parts." Life goes on. And we survive.

"People change and forget to tell each other."

Lillian Hellman

A Well-Disguised Angel

"Be miserable. Or motivate yourself. Whatever has to be done,
it is always your choice. "
Wayne Dyer

A local newspaper reporter asked me who the most influential people in my life were thus far. I gave what to me were the obvious answers: my resilient mother; my beloved Faith; Sister Florence Leone; Rabbi Raphael Levine; as well as many luminaries such as Jesus, Buddha, Gandhi, King, Emerson, Charles and Myrtle Fillmore, Ernest Holmes, and so on. Then, out of the blue, a teacher popped into my mind who had humiliated me in front of my high-school senior class. I could see his face, but I had buried his name.

As you may already know through my writings, my teen years were pretty troubled after the death of my father. After several years of getting into trouble with the law and school authorities, I had a reputation as being a "tough" guy who didn't care about much of anything. One night, sitting bloodied and battered in a jail cell, I had a vivid vision of my future, and I decided to change course. I had finally hit rock bottom. I had just turned sixteen, but that night in jail I saw very clearly that if I didn't do life differently, *this* would be my life. I was lost and alone, and that night I decided in my heart of hearts to turn things around. Without telling a soul, I went to work finding myself again. I quietly dropped "my partners in mischief" and started to apply myself to my studies with the goal of getting into college, which meant I would have to improve my grade-point average quickly to the 2.5 required to get into a state college. Over the next eighteen months, I worked hard to bring that grade point up, and I did. In my senior year, I was accepted into one of the three state colleges to which I had applied.

In the last semester of that year, a math teacher by the name of Mr. Robinette asked, "How many of you have applied to and been accepted into college?" I raised my hand with many others, and he laughed and mocked, "Moran, who do you think you are kidding? There isn't a college in the world that would accept you." As I look back, he was probably joking, but my face burned with embarrassment. The class laughed along with him, and his words kept echoing in my ears. I couldn't speak. From that day forward, whenever I attempted anything new, I would hear Mr. Robinette's words, and I would either not try at all, or I would get super determined to prove him wrong.

Mr. Robinette also had a night job as a clerk in a small grocery store. Whenever I drove by, I would see him with his apron on, hard at work late into the night. I had fantasies of one day becoming successful at something, anything, getting into his checkout line, and saying, "Do you remember me? I am the one you said would never amount to anything. Well, you were wrong, Mr. Robinette." That fantasy lasted for years, and I relished the day I would fulfill it. Eventually, it faded away, and I even forgot his name until that reporter asked me the question, and I awakened from a dream, and there he was again almost five decades later.

Now I look at Mr. Robinette differently. I feel great compassion and even gratitude for him. I will never know his story, but he must have really needed the money to work at least twelve hours every single day, year after year. Perhaps he owned that little grocery store. He didn't seem to be a happy man, but he obviously took his family responsibilities seriously, and I admire that. His motivation for saying something so seemingly unkind and demoralizing to an insecure seventeen-year-old will remain a mystery to me, but his words drove me to prove him wrong. I once heard it said that the wings of angels are often found on the backs of the least likely people. Mr. Robinette was definitely a well-disguised angel!

While I have not had great worldly success, I enjoyed the love of my soul partner for over twenty-five years and two very rich and fulfilling careers as a broadcaster and a minister. And I am super rich in friends. As strange as it may seem, Mr. Robinette turned out to be one of the most influential people in my life. It is forty-seven years late, but thank you, Mr. Robinette! I owe a great deal to you.

January 2012

"Obstacles don't have to stop you. If you run into a wall, don't turn around and give up. Figure out how to climb it, go through it, or work around it."

Michael Jordan

Our Faith Grows through Challenges

"The important thing is this: to be able at any moment to sacrifice what we are for what we may become."

Charles Dubois

I remember a most interesting conversation with a member of the congregation going through a spiritual wilderness experience. He had lost his connection with God and was feeling confused, lost, saddened, and abandoned. Have you ever felt that way? I certainly have at times.

I have come to learn that those times are common to one who is consciously evolving spiritually. As we continue to grow, experiment, observe, and experience life, our old concepts about life, ourselves, and God come into question and change or just dissolve.

I vividly recall when Faith and I were eager ministerial students, and I enthusiastically prayed, "God, I want to know You more. I am ready to remove anything from my life that stands between me and a greater awareness of You in my life." Well, as the saying goes, be careful what you ask for; within a matter of months, we were facing bankruptcy from an event over which we had no control.

Our savings were gone and, with them, our sense of security. We were forced to rely solely on God as our Source.

Now, let me emphasize: I am not saying we have a "trickster God" who was waiting for my "dare" to put me to the test. That's just superstitious nonsense many of us grew up hearing...especially those of us who are Irish. Unexpected life-altering events are a normal part of this life experience. I prayed for greater meaning, life happened, and now I had to dig deeper and reach higher than I ever had to before. My old perspective of life was gone and with it my old, comfortable concept of God. Now what?

It is when we are in the "now what?" that we grow spiritually because we have to, or we give in to despair. For me, despair wasn't a long-term option—I had a family to support. Faith and I decided to put the spiritual principles we planned to share as ministers to the test at a whole new level. If they didn't work for us during tough times, we had no intention of spreading false hope to others.

At our lowest time of faith and facing financial ruin, we kicked up our spiritual practice and began tithing for the first time in our lives, we expanded our daily times of prayer, meditation, and affirmation, and we agreed to gently redirect each other if we began to slip into fear and negativity. I would love to say that within a matter of weeks things magically turned around. Actually they got worse for a while, but I can say that within a year we were in a better place financially, and our relationships with God and with each other had grown and matured far beyond where we were at the beginning of our wilderness trek. Our faith grew even stronger over time.

These are challenging economic times for many of us, and it is also a time rich with opportunity to grow our understanding of God's presence in our lives. The old rules don't apply anymore as the world, as we have known it, shifts. We are each being called to go higher and deeper in our spiritual practice, which will lead to a greater experience of true well-being and abundance that can only be found in God.

We are all in this together, so hang in there, do your spiritual work, and leave the rest to God.

"It takes a lot of courage to release the familiar and seemingly secure, and to embrace the new. But there is no real security in what is no longer meaningful. There is more security in the exciting and adventurous, for in movement there is life, and in change, there is power."

Alan Cohen

"I Want What She's Having"

"There is very little difference in people, but that little difference makes a huge difference. The difference is attitude. The big difference is whether it is positive or negative."

W. Clement Stone

One of my favorite pastimes while traveling is to observe people in airports as they deal with the joys and stresses of air travel. Lately it seems there are more stresses than joys, but most people take it all in stride and go with the flow. On one trip to Washington, I had a couple of interesting moments as a delayed flight was announced. Most people grumbled a little bit and went about making other arrangements while a few others went ballistic and started yelling at the gate attendants, who had no power over anything. Flight delays are a part of air travel today, and those who travel regularly have learned to be flexible or go crazy.

One man in particular totally lost it and started rudely berating anyone associated with the "guilty" airline. My initial reaction was, *man, am I glad I'm not on his flight.* At first I gave him the benefit of the doubt, figuring he had a family emergency to attend to or an important business meeting. It turns out the delayed flight would put him in rush-hour traffic in Spokane, Washington. Trust me; they don't know *real* rush-hour traffic in Spokane.

I'm sure there must have been other stresses going on in his life for him to go off like that over a delay of a few hours. But he only distressed himself and those around him more with his ranting. It was interesting to watch the reactions of the other inconvenienced passengers as they registered annoyance and even anger at the "mad" man. His negativity was infecting others around him.

I was most impressed with the airline gate attendant who, I am sure, receives more than her share of tired, frustrated passengers projecting all of their annoyance onto her. She remained a center of calm and courtesy throughout the whole episode. I wasn't the only one who noticed; as the "future road-rager" stormed off, other passengers went out of their way to compliment her on her composure. I heard more than one person say something like, "How did you do that? I wish I had your composure. I wanted to slug that guy!"

Two people under stress and two totally different choices of attitude—he chose to act like an immature victim, and she chose peace and good cheer even though she was the target of his wrath. Everyone brings something to the party. I want what she's having!

February 2009

"We who lived in the concentration camps can remember the ones who walked through huts comforting others, giving away their last piece of bread. They were few in number, but they offered sufficient proof

that everything can be taken from a man but one thing: the last of his freedoms, to choose one's attitude in any given set of circumstances, to choose one's own way."

Viktor Frankl

Sacred Soul Contract

"Life is short: break the rules, forgive quickly, kiss slowly, love truly, and laugh uncontrollably. And never regret anything that made you smile."

Jack Clifford

It was just one of those nights. I had tossed and turned for hours and finally got up at 3:00 a.m. I had been struggling with the unanswerable question *"why?"* as it related to the declining health of my beautiful wife, Faith. Even my mantra of *"Peace, be still"* wouldn't keep this nagging question at bay. This was not the way we saw our lives unfolding.

Life is full of surprises, and it offers many opportunities for us to step back and say, "What the hell?" I guess it goes back to the quote by John Lennon, "Life is what happens when you make other plans." I'm not complaining, although that day I was on the verge of a major pity-party. I was just wondering, *why?* And, in my weaker moments, *does any of life really mean anything?*

The day before I had found a prayer Faith wrote in her 2004 Day-Timer right after she returned from the Mayo Clinic with her diagnosis of posterior cortical atrophy (PCA), a rare and untreatable neurological disorder. Her once distinctively beautiful handwriting was now childlike and difficult to read. This was one of the first symptoms I had noticed and finally had to admit to myself that something was terribly wrong. Here is the prayer she scribbled out and prayed to help her find her way back to center point. Even as her human self was questioning and grieving, she found comfort in her disciplined spirituality.

"Living, Loving, Sacred Presence, I surrender all of me to You. Help me to remember that You are in me and I in You. In all that I do and all that I am, may I live the purpose you have for my life and fulfill my sacred contract I made with You before my human birth."

That was such a "Faith" prayer. I turned to the next page, and she had scribbled in bold letters, *God first always.*

Faith and I always believed that we were fulfilling a sacred contract in this lifetime together. She truly believed that and so do I. I felt that way when I first met Faith and knew instantly that she was my Divine Appointment.

We naturally questioned the reasons for her illness, which came at a time in our lives when everything seemed so effortless and wonderful. After struggling with the questions, we always came back to the idea that this was part of our souls' curricula in this lifetime, and we had willingly signed on because we needed the lessons for our souls' development. I can say with certainty we both grew in many ways because of this path we chose.

That night I had been questioning whether or not we were just kidding ourselves so that we could try to bring some order and meaning to the suffering. Perhaps, but it beats endless wallowing in self-pity. I have come to believe that if you can't find meaning in something then assign meaning and purpose to it and call it good. Even though I didn't know the "whys" of all of this, I knew that Faith was right on schedule with her sacred soul contract entered into before her birth.

Just when I needed it most, my friend Jack Clifford, a cancer survivor who had found his own meaning in his search for answers to the unanswerable questions, sent this wisdom to me:

"Choose to change your habit of noticing only chaos and turmoil.
Notice God instead.
In the middle of a crisis notice God's love in your heart.
Notice God's breath in your lungs, God's song on your lips, and God's joy in your soul.
See God's infinite love shining out of the eyes of another.
Wherever you are, God is.
Every moment holds the gift of peace. Choose to accept it.
Every sixty seconds you choose to spend upset is a minute you will never get back.
Life may not be the party we hoped for, but while we are here, let's dance..."

October 2007

Living Fully

*"Live as if you were to die tomorrow. Learn as if you were to
live forever."*

Gandhi

In February several years ago, one of my very best friends died. He
was my brother...my soul brother. His name is Rory Elder, and he
and his wife, Vicky, had been Anam Caras (soul friends) of Faith's
and mine for many years. I vividly remember the first time we met
the Elders. Faith and I had started working as associate ministers at
Christ Unity Church in Sacramento, and Rory and Vicky (Ro and
Vic) were counselors associated with the church. Everybody we
met kept telling us we had to meet the Elders and that we would
love them.

We were leaving the church office one day as they were pull-
ing into the parking lot. They jumped out of their car and rushed
over to introduce themselves. Vicky was (still is) tall and pretty
with a huge smile. Rory was a big bear of a man who could over-
power you with his effusive energy, good cheer, and endless stream
of words, which poured non-stop from him. I have never known

anyone who enjoyed words and word play as much. He was the "Prince of Puns."

At first I didn't know what to make of him. He felt too big, too full of love, too supportive, and too full of admiration to be real. But the longer I knew Ro and Vic, the more I came to realize there really are people who are exactly as they present themselves. The Elders became two of our dearest friends with whom we shared the many ups and downs of life as parents, friends, students, and co-ministers. We spent many rich hours in conversation or just hanging out and being there for each other. That's what I loved most about them, just hanging out and being present for each other and not having to be any way other than how we were at that moment. Ro and I could say or do anything without fear of being judged or rejected by the other, and, before long, we would be poking fun at each other and roaring with laughter. That's what I miss the most, the safety of his friendship and the belly laughs.

Vicky reminded me that Ro and I had made an agreement long ago to perform the memorial service for the one who "went" first. I remembered making that agreement, but at the time it seemed such a long way off, and I never gave it a second thought. I was honored to officiate at his memorial service but was nervous about doing it because my feelings were so raw. While sitting at my desk, praying and thinking about Rory and Vicky, my eyes went to a piece of sage that Rory had given me when the two of us led the memorial service for another great friend, Cruz Azevedo. Rory and Cruz both shared Native-American blood. Cruz was a pipe carrier for the Yaqui Nation, and Rory was a member of the Choctaw tribe. They were two of a kind...wise and wacky! I remembered Rory lighting the sage and performing a cleansing and blessing ceremony as he chanted prayers for Cruz at his service. Over the years, I had watched Cruz do similar ceremonies many times at Spiritual Life Center.

That morning I lit the sage in their honor, inhaled its sweetness, and sent up my prayers for them with the smoke. Through my tears I could feel a sense of inner joy and absolute faith in knowing they are as alive today as they ever have been or ever will be. I swear I could hear them chanting and dancing and laughing and calling out to me. I still can...right now, as I write this.

The service was as big and wonderful as Ro. It began with chanting of prayers and drumming and shaking of the rattles to alert Great Spirit and Mother Earth that their son was coming home. The Native-American flute soothed our grieving hearts, and the sweet smell of white sage burning helped cleanse us of any negative energy. Rory's service was filled with rivers of tears and oceans of laughter. It reflected the impact one person can have on a community. His two sons gave the most moving tribute to a father I have ever heard. I used to envy the natural, easygoing relationships he had with his sons, Travis and Kyle. One thing almost every person who spoke mentioned was how Ro made you feel like you were the most important person in the world, deserving of his full attention. It was one big *wow!*

The tears I shed are not for Rory (trust me, he's doing just fine!); they are for those of us left behind, especially Vicky, his wife and soul mate; sons, Kyle and Travis; and daughter, Brianna.

Ro loved his family and friends above all else, and he went out of his way to lavish his love and appreciation on us. Rory was a bright light, and his leaving has taken some of the brightness out of the world. This is the opportunity for us to crank up our own lives and lights to help illuminate our beautiful and troubled world.

Jack Kornfield, the American Buddhist writer, says, "At the end of your life you will be asked just two questions:

1) Did you live your life fully?
2) Did you love lavishly?"

If you were asked these questions today, how would you truthfully respond? Well, this is your life...it is never too late to *live fully and love lavishly!*

February 2007

"You would know the secret of death. But how shall you find it unless you seek it in the heart of life? If you would indeed behold the spirit of death, open your heart wide unto the joy of life. For life and death are one, even as the river and the seas are one."

Khalil Gibran

Gratitude in the Present Moment

"Nobody can go back and start a new beginning, but anyone can start today and make a new ending."

Maria Robinson

I walk almost every day along the levee near my home with three friends whom I call my "peeps." We have done this for years, and there is very little we haven't shared with one another. We have built up a high level of comfort and trust that can only be achieved by consistently being there for one another. We show up, we listen, support, and challenge each other, hold each other accountable, sometimes just walk silently, and most often wind up laughing uproariously over one of our foibles. I consider them to be among my most treasured gifts.

This morning it was just Mike Z and me, or "the Mikes," as we are known at Cafe Latte, where we go after our morning walk. We get our beverage, a bagel or a muffin to share, and sit and talk some more. Our early-morning routine is almost ritualistic, and it has come to feel sacred. I love it and miss it when I am out of town or unable to show up for one reason or another.

This morning as we walked it was picture-perfect; the silvery moon was full and bright, moon shadows stretched out before us, and it was very still, until we were visited by two vocal owls who flew over and landed high in a tree right next to us. I always feel blessed by owls and feel they are trying to convey something important to me. Mike and I stopped and listened and called back to them for a period of time.

When we resumed our magical walk, I asked Mike, "What was the happiest time in your life? You know, the time when everything seemed to be just right?" I had been thinking about that because I had recently uncovered pictures of me with Faith, when we were so happy and in love. Mike thought for a long time before he answered, and then he said, "Back there, when we stood there in the presence of those owls, and walking with you now along the levee."

His comment spurred an insightful discussion about how we tend to look to the distant past for the happiest times, and we often fail to notice the beauty, joy, and wonder that surround us in every present moment. It was true: in that moment we were totally present, we were not missing anything or anyone, worrying about our health, careers, the past or future, or relationships. It was as close to bliss as one can get, and it was so simple. That feeling of contentment stayed with me all day.

My challenge to you, and to me, is to make the time to stop, see, and listen to the rhythm and wonder of life. When was the last time you consciously took in the awe and wonder of this amazing world and life? Today I did, and it made this the first day of the best days of the rest of my life.

November 2009

"No matter where I am, no matter what my circumstances are, no matter whether my life is fun or hard, no matter what I have or don't have; if I learn to listen to my life, and see God in my everyday trivialities, transformation happens. I start seeing the world, God, others and myself for who we really are. Ordinary becomes special, and the lost sense of wonder, joy and mystery is rediscovered."

Frederick Buechner

When Life Brings You to Your Knees
Radical Generosity

"Whatever you do for the least of these my brothers and sisters, you do for me."
Rabbi Jesus

In August of 2008, I had the pleasure of officiating at the wedding of Carrie Shellhammer and Zachary Chown under the redwoods in beautiful Truckee, California. This wedding was especially sweet for me because, five years earlier, Faith and I had visited Carrie as she lay dying in a San Francisco hospital. Two months before that visit, Faith had been diagnosed with her terminal illness.

Carrie had come to us in 2002 and asked for prayers and spiritual guidance as she was waiting for the double-lung transplant that could save her life. It was heartbreaking to witness this intelligent, beautiful young woman pour out her longing for the life she was afraid she would never live. Faith and I connected with Carrie immediately. She became our special friend and prayer focus. We helplessly watched her health decline as the clock ticked. Faith told Carrie to live her life as if she had all the time in the world. She gave her an angel to keep with her to remind her of God's love and Faith's faith in her.

When we left Carrie after our last hospital visit, she was extremely weak and close to death. We expected our next visit would be with her family to arrange her memorial service. Carrie and her mother, Chris, had already chosen the songs for her service, "Blackbird, Born to Fly" and "You Can Close Your Eyes." We were dreading what looked to be inevitable. It seemed so unfair.

But Carrie is alive today because of the radical generosity of her donor's family, her faith, her will to live, and the wonders of medical science. There wasn't a dry eye in the group as she walked down the aisle to the song "At Last." Not only was Carrie getting married and diving into the life she once feared lived only in her imagination, another young man named Matt, who had received the same donor's heart a few hours before Carrie received the gift of healthy lungs, was watching alongside his new wife of three months. Blessed are those who give and receive.

It was a *wow* moment for all of us: two young people who would be dead now if it weren't for the decision of the donor's family to honor their loved one's brief life and tragic death by giving total strangers the gift of a second chance. The donor lives on through Carrie and Matt and who knows how many others.

By the way, the songs Carrie had chosen for her memorial service were played at her wedding, as well as "What a Wonderful World" in memory of Faith.

In the United States there are nearly 100,000 people waiting for organ transplants. Eighteen die every day. If you would like to offer a second chance of life to another, consider registering with the Transplant Donor Network in your state. It takes about five minutes. Five minutes could be that second chance for someone else.

August 2008

"Go confidently in the direction of your dreams. Live the life you have imagined!"

Henry David Thoreau

When Forgiveness Seems Impossible

"Experience: the most brutal of all teachers. But you learn, my God, do you learn!"

C.S. Lewis

A man came into my office saddened over a betrayal he had suffered at the hands of a friend he trusted and loved. Every betrayal begins with trust and love. It is a story as old as humankind. We all have been "sold out" at one time or another, and, if we are honest, we have probably deliberately or inadvertently betrayed another's trust in some way, and they suffered because of it. Both sides of betrayal suffer.

Betrayal is a part of life that few of us, if any, escape. Betrayal by a trusted friend or spouse can seem overwhelming. It is hard to imagine what someone thinks they can gain by trying to ruin your reputation, betraying your confidence, or selfishly risking your heart for their own interests. It ranks as one of the most painful experiences we will ever face, but how we choose to deal with it determines the difference between you and the betrayer. How someone treats you is their Karma, and how you respond to them, in turn, determines yours.

The man in my office felt stuck, angry, and humiliated; he kept replaying in his mind what he could possibly have done to deserve such seemingly cruel and unjust treatment. He could not seem to get clear of the unfairness of the situation, and there seemed to be no way to resolve it. Now what?

One of the hard spiritual truths we must embrace is, "It is never about them." Now, this doesn't mean that they didn't do something that deeply wounded you and that they shouldn't be held accountable. It does mean now that it has occurred, *you* are the only one who can resolve it. You are the only one who can find peace again. It is all about you now and how you choose to respond.

I wish I had a way to avoid all the pain of recovery, but I don't. It is one of those messy things we each have to deal with now and then—broken vows or confidences, gossip, lies, infidelities, and so on. I gently advise people to genuinely "feel" the pain, cry yourself empty, shout yourself hoarse, seek help from a professional if it is beyond your ability to move on, and always turn to God. There is no way around betrayal, only through it. At some point you will want to forgive, but first you must truly feel before you can authentically heal.

The only things that have helped me are to seek clarity and peace from God and to remind myself I will survive this. Not only that, but, with God's help, I will do all I can to thrive because of this betrayal. I tell myself I will look for and accept the blessing this "horribly wrapped gift" contains for me. I tell myself that I will not insult the dignity of my soul by seeking vengeance and acting in kind. I can only heal and thrive if I choose to take the high road and not play in the same dark, murky energy of the betrayer.

I have also discovered that if I have excessive energy about the "deed done to me," it is sometimes because I have not yet forgiven myself for having done a similar deed to someone else. For instance, a friend of mine was raging about a promise someone wasn't keeping with her until she remembered she still harbored guilt at having broken her promise of fidelity to her former husband. Once she realized the connection, she stopped judging the other person so harshly, the energy and upset about the current broken promise dissipated, and she was able to more rationally reach resolution with the current situation.

I also remind myself nobody...*nobody*...escapes from "Captain Karma," including me. I have often found as I move along the road of healing that I eventually come to appreciate the "betrayers" because of the spiritual and emotional growth that comes out of the incident. At that point, I can actually bless them and wish only healing for their souls. It is a slow process, but if we position ourselves on the side of "positive possibility," we always grow spiritually. *Everything* that happens in our lives is for our spiritual growth. I believe that is why our souls volunteered for this human experience. The great mystic poet Rumi stated, "Even if they're a crowd of sorrows, who violently sweep your house empty of its furniture, still, treat each guest honorably. They may be clearing you out for some new delight."

November 2009

"Whatever relationships you have attracted into your life at this moment, are precisely the ones you need in your life at this moment. There is a hidden meaning in all events, and this hidden meaning is serving your own evolution."

Dr. Deepak Chopra

Metaphorical Storms

"Once you choose hope, anything is possible."
Christopher Reeve

It was a cool, blustery, rainy day. The rain was pounding on my roof, skylight, and patio; the wind was howling and whipping the trees back and forth; leaves were cascading down, and dead branches were hitting my roof and filling the yard. Mother Nature was doing some long-overdue housecleaning. Days like this are among my favorites. I was home, it was a day off, and I could sit back, relax, and enjoy the first major storm of fall. I was in for the day, cuddled up with a good book and a couple of films on DVD.

I turned on the television to get the latest news about the storm and realized not everyone was enjoying Mother Nature's cleansing frenzy as I was. People were tied up in traffic jams; large tree limbs had fallen on houses, cars, and power lines, knocking out electricity in many parts of the city. While I was in a wee bit of heaven, others were in a soggy, frustrating hell. Same storm, very different experiences.

As the storm raged on, I found my mind wandering all over the place. I felt compassion for the homeless who had inadequate clothing and no place to go for shelter, and the birds and other animals that had to hunker down and endure the discomfort of the storm. I also thought about how good it must be for the trees to be getting a thorough washing and pruning, how the thirsty earth was soaking up the fresh water, and how clean the air and everything else would be after the storm passed.

My mind wandered to the metaphorical storms that occasionally blow through each of our lives and shake up everything. A couple of years ago a woman told me of one such "life storm" that had completely shaken up every aspect of her "secure" life. She lost her job of eleven years and was forced to find occasional temporary work to make ends meet. The man of her dreams chose to end the relationship and moved on. The condo they had shared for over five years was being sold, and she had to move elsewhere within a month. She kept crying, "Why me?"

She was devastated, but we prayed together that good would come from it even though she could not see it at the time. I would talk to her on the phone during her worst times and encourage her to keep hope alive. She prayed and prayed, and things got much worse. Broke and alone, she had to leave the area to live with a younger sister who reluctantly offered to take her in until she got back on her feet. She found herself in a strange new state with no friends, feeling like a "capital-L Loser" (her words). But she kept praying and affirming that good would come to her.

A little over two years later, she credits the "storm" for shaking her up enough that she had to make some dramatic new choices. Little by little her life took on a whole new direction. She is now managing a successful local business in her new hometown. Her new boss so appreciates and depends on her he advanced her a down payment on a beautiful home to ensure she would stay. The forced living arrangement with her sister enabled them to heal some old family wounds that had alienated them from one another most of their lives. She is surrounded by new friends, a spiritual community she enjoys, and she has released the forty pounds she gained during the stormy period. When I asked her if there was any romance in her new life, she laughed and said, "No, I don't worry about that. It will happen if it happens."

By the way, the prayer she prayed through all of the stormy change was "Thank You, God. Good is all around me, and I am at peace. I am blessed with all I need."

"I know God will not give me anything I can't handle. I just wish that He didn't trust me so much."

Mother Teresa

Will Grief Heal Me? The Journey from Awful to Awe-filled

"There is a sacredness in tears. They are not the mark of weakness, but of power. They speak more eloquently than ten thousand tongues. They are the messengers of overwhelming grief...and unspeakable love."

Washington Irving

Let us talk about loss and grieving. Something wonderful has been happening to me lately that I find to be very life-affirming. People have been saying things to me like, "You've changed; you look lighter; you seem happier. It feels like the old you is back!" It is true—I feel as if I am finally emerging from a long, dark, and narrow tunnel. Faith, my wife, lover, best friend, and partner in ministry for twenty-five years, has been gone almost eighteen months. Her disease and prolonged dying process took me to dark, lonely places I would never have consciously chosen to go—nobody would. As I have stated before, "I would not wish the experience on my worst enemy, nor would I trade the sacred journey we walked together for all the riches in the world. It was a journey from awful to awe-filled."

In my lifetime, I have lost many friends and beloved family members, but Faith's death was much more soul-wrenching. The grieving process was more intense than I thought it could possibly be. The words of the writer of Psalm 31:9 touched me deeply during that awful period: *"Be merciful to me, O Lord, for I am in great distress; my eyes grow weak with sorrow, my soul and body with grief."* Anyone who has suffered great loss knows that feeling all too well.

The grieving continues for me but no longer in an all-consuming way. When I recently explained this to a friend, he asked, "How is it different now?" I heard myself say, "Well, I still think of Faith many times every day, but now I don't think of her every single minute of every single day." For a while I felt guilty because I feared I was losing the memory of her, but Faith is such an integral part of who I am that to forget her would be impossible.

Death and loss are a part of every life, and it doesn't matter whether it is our parents, siblings, friends, beloved pets, a divorce, or loss of love, job, or health; the pain and shock of it are always there, but over time they gradually fade to a tolerable level. As promised by the sages of the ages, the long, dark night of the soul will eventually give way to the bright light of a new day. It takes time for grief to transform us, but transform us it does, if we surrender to it and let the pain, despair, and tears wash over us. Good grief heals us.

The grieving process is different for everyone. I know for myself the grieving seemed unbearable for so long, and some people found my process so tedious and uncomfortable that they left. A few well-intentioned people stated, "It has been long enough now, and it is time for you to get over it and get on with life." They wanted the old me back. Trust me, I wanted that, too, but that person didn't exist anymore. You see, grieving transforms us into someone else entirely. As we journey along this uncharted territory, we learn to peacefully coexist side by side with loss and pain and joy and gratitude. We emerge with greater depth, more compassion, a much deeper appreciation for life, and less attachment to the opinions of others. The goal is not to be the way we were before the loss but to become *more* than we were.

If you are mourning the loss of someone or something precious to you, I can now speak with some deeper personal experience—pray, be patient with yourself and others who can't know, cry yourself dry, talk yourself empty, surround yourself with supportive listeners who fan the flames of hope, and get help if you are completely mired in the intensity of the pain. The great American poet Robert Frost said, "In three words I can sum up everything I have learned about life: It goes on."

Yes, it does, and I am so grateful. Thank You, God!

June 2009

"Grief shared is grief diminished."

Rabbi Grollman

An Authentic Sermon

"If you call forth that which is within you, it will save you. If you do not call forth that which is within you, it will destroy you."

Gnostic Gospel of Thomas

I really struggled with continuing in ministry without Faith serving at my side on a daily basis. I had no framework of ministry without her as my equal partner. We had been in this together from the conception of the idea of an Interfaith Unity Ministry while picnicking on the banks of Glacier Creek near the Washington-Canadian border in 1980. On that bright (and rare) warm, sunny afternoon, we actually "saw" what became Spiritual Life Center about eighteen years before that wonderful community physically arrived. When we did come together in 1998 at the Radisson Hotel, it was like a family reunion, and together we launched Spiritual Life Center. Faith said many times, "We have all been together before, and now we have come together again to finish the work we left undone." It always felt like that to me as well. We truly were all called together by Divine Appointment to accomplish a noble purpose.

We used to joke that, between the two of us, Faith and I made one very good minister. It was true! Her gifts of organization, personnel skills, community-building, peace-making, and humble, love-centered service complemented my gifts perfectly. She was always my teacher and reference point as to how to do small things with great love and absolute spiritual integrity.

Faith and I have been soul partners ever since we met, and I believe even before that. I remember dropping her off at her condominium after our first date and rushing home to call a friend who lived in Chicago (3:00 a.m. her time) to tell her I had just met the woman I was going to marry. My attitude before that night was that I was happily single and intended to stay that way. I don't know how I knew without a doubt that Faith was the "perfect" one for me, but I just *knew* to the core of my being she was my long-awaited Anam Cara (soul friend). She appealed to me on every level. I spent the next two hours telling my friend about Faith and how she was different than any woman I had ever known...blah, blah, blah. My friend patiently listened (or slept) as I rambled on. That's what friends are for...right?

You would think we would get married and live happily ever after, but real life isn't so neat and tidy. It took two to three years of rich inner work, including painful separations, before we each felt whole and healthy enough to do marriage differently than we each had previously. Faith often informed me that God would always be number one in her life and that I would always be second.

Our lives totally changed when Faith's diagnosis and illness forced her to retire. Together, we grieved the loss of our ministerial relationship and the many other ways life drastically changed for us. For months we grieved...and celebrated each day we still had together. On Sundays, Faith did her best to "suit up and show up" for as long as possible, even when she worried she might do it "wrong." We, her friends and family, would all hold our collective breath, wondering if she would make it through the greeting. I marveled at her courage (or stubbornness) and willingness to get back up and try again week after week. Some people wondered why I let her struggle on as long as I did before shifting her from what was obviously an uncomfortable and stressful situation for her and many of us as well. It was because it was so important to her, and I felt I owed it to her as the heart and founding minister of SLC to allow her to minister as best she could for as long as she could. Did I let it go on too long? Possibly. If she were not my wife and partner in ministry, would I have allowed her to continue? Probably not.

Folks, this was real life. Life is rarely neat and tidy with Hollywood beginnings, middles, and endings. In our culture, too often we try to cover up or hide those among us who are afflicted and struggling because it makes us feel uncomfortable or anxious. But that is not real life, is it? Spiritual Life Center was created to teach spiritual principles and practices that empower us to be authentic, not pretend, people.

When Faith stood up there, shaking, stuttering, or groping for words, it was an authentic sermon on courage, willingness, openness, and absence of ego. I personally could not have done it as long as Faith did because I am way too self-conscious, and I wouldn't want anyone to see me that vulnerable and open to others' judgments. Each time I watched her attempt it, one more time with varying results, I felt nervous and also proud of her and greatly inspired. I hope to be more like her someday.

One Sunday a woman approached me after watching Faith have a particularly difficult time, and she said, "You know, I come here every Sunday, and I get two sermons: the one you give, which I enjoy, and the one Faith gives by just showing up, and that's the one I never forget. I *always* remember *her* sermons."

She was right on the money—your life, my life are our only true sermons. Life is rarely like a beautifully delivered sermon or a well-rehearsed and choreographed musical. Real life is how we "suit up and show up" every day. We always strove to minister in the most honest and authentic way possible, even when it didn't measure up to "show-biz" standards. In many of Faith's former Sunday lessons, she often said, "I am here to comfort the afflicted and afflict the comfortable." And so she did.

I encourage each of us to "keep the Faith." May we each be willing to accept the life we have, be grateful for it, live it boldly, love lavishly, and do those things we feel are beneath us with great love, humility, and joy. Remember, your life is the only authentic sermon you will ever deliver.

January 2007

"Everybody can be great...because anybody can serve. You don't have to have a college degree to serve. You don't need to make your subject and verb agree to serve. You only need a heart full of grace. A soul generated by love."

Rev. Dr. Martin Luther King, Jr.

Losing Someone to Suicide

"There is no death! What seems so is transition; this life of mortal breath is but a suburb of the life Elysian, whose portal we call death."

Henry W. Longfellow

One day several years ago, I received news that felt like a sudden hard blow to my heart; it literally took my breath away. I was told a friend I greatly liked and admired had taken his own life. That was the last thing I would have expected to hear about him. Just weeks earlier, I had spoken with him about a project he would design and oversee for the remodel at our new facility. He seemed upbeat, energized, and full of life at that time. As I absorbed the news, I felt a wave of conflicting emotions course through me— shock, sadness, anger, compassion, guilt, bewilderment, and concern for his family. My inner voice kept repeating, "How could this happen; what did I miss?"

This was not the first suicide of someone I have known. As a minister of twenty-five years, I have officiated at memorial services for suicide victims and ministered to their families as they dealt with the aftermath and descended into the depths of unimaginable grief. Grieving a death is difficult enough, but suicide grief is in a category all its own. It never gets easier for me. The last person I would have expected to die this way was my friend. I have always looked up to him because he had overcome many major hardships in life that most of us can't even imagine. My life issues seemed minuscule next to his, and he rarely, if ever, complained. I still admire his strength of character, good nature, and resolve to not let his physical limitations prevent him from experiencing life to its fullest.

So what happened? We will probably never know, but I can only surmise he was beset by an inner enemy and sense of hopelessness that was very real to him. In that darkness, he chose what he perceived was the only way out. I pray that none of us will ever know the depth of despair he must have experienced to have chosen this solution to what had to seem an unsolvable dilemma. I don't blame or judge him at all. I just miss him and wish I could have talked with him before he made his final decision. I am bothered that he felt so alone when so many of us loved and cared for him.

Many times the families or friends of suicide victims share with me their fears that their loved one's soul is in jeopardy because the religion of their childhood impressed upon them that those who choose "this way out" are eternally condemned. I was taught that as a child, and even then it seemed inconsistent with a God of unconditional love. I vividly remember thinking as a child of eight or nine, why would God condemn someone who was already sick and hurting so much? My child's sense of fairness couldn't believe in a vindictive, mean-spirited God. I still can't or won't.

Here is what I believe: every soul is precious and wanted. My friend died of a disease called depression. Depression, just like some forms of cancer, diabetes, or heart disease, can be managed, but it can also claim one's life if it gets out of control. We rarely blame sufferers of cancer or heart disease for their deaths, unless they were reckless with their lifestyles. We usually express great compassion and say, "Well, at least now they are free of their suffering." That is how I feel when I hear of a suicide. I feel sadness and compassion. I have an image of the tired and despondent soul being compassionately embraced and lovingly comforted by the Divine Presence, just as any parent would gently hold and reassure a confused, frightened, and hurting child. I trust the God of my understanding is incapable of turning away from or rejecting one of Its own because the child has become frightened, disoriented, and lost its way.

To my friend I say, "Godspeed on your new soul adventure, and thank you for touching my life in ways you probably never knew. You always inspired me to stop making excuses and at least try something new and challenging." To his family and friends, I pray we all experience the promise of "the peace that passes all human understanding." To those reading this, I urge us all to take the time to listen more carefully to our families and friends as we examine our relationships with them more closely and treasure our time together more dearly.

October 2010

"Do not stand at my grave and weep, I am not there, I do not sleep.
I am a thousand winds that blow; I am the softly falling snow.
I am the gentle showers of rain; I am the fields of ripening grain.
I am in the morning hush; I am in the graceful rush

Of beautiful birds in circling flight. I am the starshine of the night.
I am in the flowers that bloom, I am in a quiet room.
I am in the birds that sing, I am in each lovely thing.
Do not stand at my grave and cry, I am not there—I do not die."

Mary Elizabeth Frye

Accepting What Washes Up on Your Beach

"We ask 'why did this happen?' At some point, why it is here doesn't really matter. It has washed up on my beach and it is mine to deal with. The only question for me now is, 'Who do I choose to become as I walk this new path life has put before me?'"

Faith Moran

Shortly after we received Faith's diagnosis in October of 2003, we shared the news with our congregation. Here is a portion of her letter she read to them:

"For the past two to three years, I have been experiencing neurological problems which have affected my speaking skills and ability to focus. The symptoms would come and go... At first it was diagnosed as a stroke or possibly M.S. This has been difficult for me, and at times embarrassing and frightening. I wish it were different but I accept it and will move forward with great faith, knowing I will be guided to find the path of healing that is right for me. I am confident I will be given the strength and clarity to move through this with courage and grace.

"I have often called Spiritual Life Center a laboratory for spiritual growth. Well, this is a grand opportunity to demonstrate our beliefs! I believe all things work together

117

for good for those who love God, and this is no exception. This is life in its 'all-ness.' In the human condition, it is not what happens to us that matters, but who we become in the process that really matters. I will not miss the opportunity this condition offers me and our community.

"You are my spiritual family and I love you all dearly, and I love and trust God. Remember, all is well with my soul!"

Faith was and still remains my greatest teacher of *big love*. She was "good to the core," and her goodness, integrity, and love made me and everyone who ever knew her a better person. Her life was anything but easy, especially in her early years when she suffered emotional and physical abuse and humiliation. As a result, she fought low self-esteem all of her life, but she never used it as an excuse to not try the "impossible" or to stop loving God, people, and life. Instead, she somehow became more determined not to let her difficult growing-up years determine her future. The experiences that would have hardened many others tenderized her heart. She often told me that she just wanted to help people "not hurt so much." This was especially true for children.

The last five years of Faith's life were agonizing and at the same time richly rewarding as we traveled the spiritual journey of her illness together. Although I wouldn't wish this time on my worst enemy, I also would not have traded it for anything, if that makes any sense.

Faith passed away on January 17, 2008. Her Celebration of Life was attended by over one thousand friends and family. We filled the beautiful and historic church to overflowing. Spiritual leaders from Hindu, Buddhist, Jewish, Christian, Muslim, and New Thought faiths lit their faith candles from the flame of the Oneness Candle and shared a prayerful thought from their religious traditions. It was a sacred, transformative moment, and it was absolutely silent...until a small child's voice, in a stage whisper, called out, "Why is it so quiet in here?" Healing laughter erupted, and it became even more sacred and transformative. I'm certain Faith put that little "angel" up to that. She would not have allowed such a solemn celebration service to continue.

All evening I could feel Faith beaming down on us. This humble woman never had even the slightest clue of the enormous impact she had on people. Her spirit and vision will continue to guide our church along the path of peace and service. We have just begun to "love, serve, and remember," which is part of the church mission statement Faith helped to create.

Faith often quoted Pierre Teilhard de Chardin, who said, "Joy is the infallible sign of the presence of God." God and joy and Faith were certainly present at her memorial and in all of our hearts. One of the things I miss the most about her is the lilting sound of her laughter as she talked with friends and co-workers. Her laugh always lightened my day and made me smile. (I'm smiling now as I write this.) Often when we would attend interfaith gatherings, she would turn to me, smile, and quote Psalm 133, "Behold, how good and pleasant it is when brothers and sisters dwell together in unity." It was so true on that, her sacred and joyous night.

January 2008

"There are only two ways to live your life. One is as though nothing is a miracle. The other is as though everything is a miracle."

Albert Einstein

How Did I Get Here...Again?
Seeing is Believing

"If you seek greatness, forget greatness, and ask for truth and you will find both."
Hawthorne

Years ago I was given some of the most valuable advice I have ever received. I don't recall who gave it to me or even what the advice was concerning; I just remember the words, "Close your ears and open your eyes." I cannot tell you how many times that sage advice has saved me.

I have shared it many times with those seeking spiritual guidance when they are stuck in a relationship or situation that is harmful, confusing, or painful. For instance, a woman came to me repeatedly over the pain she was feeling because of a husband who alternated between being verbally abusive, demeaning her in front of friends, and withdrawing all attention if she expressed her hurt.

After hearing different versions of the same story for years, I once again asked her why she continued to put up with the heartbreak and pain. She said, "Because he is my best friend, and I know he loves me. He tells me he can't live without me." She went on to say, "I want to believe him when he says he will change and be nicer."

I handed her a page with the best description ever written of how true love actually appears. I am sure you will recognize it. It begins by saying talk is cheap. "If I speak in the tongues of men and angels, but have not love, I am only a resounding gong or clanging symbol." The writer of First Corinthians 13 (Paul) was reminding us words are easy to say, but unless they are followed by authentic action, they are just annoying noise. *Close your ears and open your eyes.*

Genuine love shows up like this:

"Love is patient, love is kind. It is not boastful and proud. It is never rude or self-seeking, it is not easily angered, and it keeps no account of past wrongs. Love does not take delight in spreading falsehood, but rejoices with the truth. Love always protects, always trusts, always hopes, always perseveres."

The Apostle Paul and I disagree on many things, but on this we couldn't be more aligned. The next time you are wondering how truly loving you or another is, *close your ears and open your eyes.* Measure the words against action. In the words of another wise man, Forrest Gump, "Love is as love does." And that's the Truth!

May 2008

"Honesty and transparency make you vulnerable. Be honest and transparent anyway."

Mother Teresa

Are You Holding On to Resentments?

"Blessed are the peacemakers for they shall be called children of God."
Rabbi Jesus

One evening while I was having a dinner-table conversation with a friend, he brought up an incident that had occurred over a decade before, when I had disappointed him in some way. I honestly had no recollection of the incident, but I apologized because I could see it bothered him enough that he felt it necessary to mention it after all those years.

After I apologized, we began a discussion over how we tend to hang on to resentments and perceived wrongs, as if doing so will somehow reap a positive result or solve anything. Most of the time we add the resentment to our evidence file and use it as an excuse for our behavior. In his powerful and fun little book *The Great Divorce*, C.S. Lewis calls our evidence file "souvenirs of hell." I love that description because each time we recall the incident, we get to revisit hell. We lose our peace.

My friend had let a perceived "slight" interfere with our relationship for a decade, and I never gave it the first thought—I never even knew. If he had risked mentioning it ten years earlier, he would have opened the possibility for us to reconcile then and saved himself many painful moments in hell. As I recalled his experience with me, I pondered how many little things I have stubbornly held on to, expecting the "other" to reach out first for reconciliation. I am sure we all have our own evidence file that needs purging.

In every wedding ceremony Faith and I performed, we shared a beautiful prayer/poem by James Dillet Freeman called "A Blessing for a Marriage." One of the lines often jumps out at me and sometimes gets caught in my throat. It says, "...and if at times we have quarrels that push us apart, may both of us have the good sense to take the first step back." That first step is the one that moves us out of hell and gets us back on the path to heaven.

Is there someone toward whom you hold a grudge or resentment? Practice being a peacemaker. Be the one to take the first step back. It is the only way to give peace a chance. Even if they don't respond in a positive way, you will have the satisfaction of knowing you have done your part to help create a more peaceful world. Let there be peace on earth and let it begin with me... and you.

November 2006

"Holding on to anger, resentment and hurt only gives you tense muscles, a headache and a sore jaw from clenching your teeth. Forgiveness gives you back the laughter and the lightness in your life."

Joan Lunden

Trapped by Memories

"The curious paradox is that when I accept myself just as I am, then I can change."

Dr. Carl Rogers

How much of what we do and what we believe about the world is the result of some long-forgotten occurrence or conditioning? One evening I watched a foreign film called *Don't Tell* that stayed with me long after the credits rolled. It is about a brother and sister who grew up together in Italy, but as adults they lived on different continents and rarely communicated with one another, even though they loved one another. They each became successful in their professions, the brother as a college professor and the sister as a voice-over actress for films. Unbeknownst to the other, each also experienced difficulties connecting with the people they loved most. Sister and brother each felt anxious, unworthy, and dissatisfied when a significant relationship was called to go deeper and be more intimate.

Finally, the younger sister had an extremely disturbing recurring dream that led her to the United States to reconnect with her brother, who was now married and had two young sons. He loved his boys dearly but wouldn't express his affection physically with hugs. She sensed that her brother might hold the key to her nightmares.

Not surprisingly, it turned out both brother and sister had been sexually abused and betrayed by their father and also their mother, who had looked the other way. Each carried the horrible secret locked away in a dark place within. When a moment of true intimacy presented itself for either of them, the old unconscious fears would surface and prevent them from fully embracing the moment. They each lived half-lives, afraid to go beyond a certain invisible, yet definite, boundary. (Push pause.)

Years ago, the National Zoo in Washington, DC, had a rare white tiger named Mohini. She lived in a twelve-foot-by-twelve-foot cage with iron bars and a cement floor. She spent her long and dreary days pacing in her cramped quarters. Finally, someone with authority and a modicum of compassion decided to offer Mohini a more natural habitat. It covered several acres and had hills, trees, a pond, and grassy areas. The news media and public excitedly awaited the day Mohini would be released and finally roam "free." On the appointed day, as the cameras rolled, Mohini was released, and she immediately retreated to a corner of her new refuge, where she lived for the remainder of her life pacing in that corner until an area twelve-foot-by-twelve-foot was worn bare. She was trapped by her past experience and memories.

The reason I share these two examples is because, unlike Mohini, the brother and sister were finally able to recognize they were keeping themselves trapped by their suppressed memories, unconscious habits, and fears. With the help of therapy, each other, and friends, they began the slow journey back to freedom. Little by little, they accepted the horrible past, put it behind them, and could then expand their territory and live fuller lives. They were able to unlearn the old patterns that had once protected them but were now sabotaging their happiness. With knowledge, they could change their mistaken beliefs that they had done something wrong.

I think perhaps the greatest human tragedy is that too many of us retreat to well-worn patterns that keep us small while a whole world of possibilities is well within our reach. What in your life is keeping you trapped?

Be willing to take a look at areas of your life and identify one where you keep repeating unhealthy patterns for no good reason. Recognizing a self-limiting pattern is half the solution. The next step is to follow the example of the younger sister in our story. She boldly (with knees knocking, I'm sure) confronted her nightmare and began the process of awakening to a larger life experience.

May 2007

"You cannot get free of a situation until you get free in it."

Rev. Faith Moran

The Serenity of Forgiveness

"May you never forget what is worth remembering, nor ever remember what is best forgotten."

Irish blessing

One of my favorite cartoons shows Charlie Brown standing on top of Snoopy's doghouse with his arms outstretched and his mouth wide open as he looks up at the vastness of the night sky, shouting, "God, I love all humanity; it is people I can't stand....augghhh!"

Haven't we all felt that way at one time or another? Charlie had probably just had another run-in with his nemesis, Lucy, and his faith in all things human was challenged. Being kind, loving, civil, compassionate, and "spiritual" would be so much easier if only we didn't have to deal with certain people...and you know who they are in your life.

Recently, I was feeling very centered and peaceful and just loving life in general, and then...I unexpectedly encountered one of *those* people in my life, and my sense of serenity went south in the blink of an eye. Suddenly my heart started racing, my mind started up its monkey-chattering, and I was mentally rehearsing what I would have said, could have said, and will say the next time. My inner atmosphere suddenly changed from sunny and clear to overcast with major storm warnings.

Fortunately, I caught myself fairly quickly, and the thought crossed my mind, *Gee, where did that peaceful, spiritual guy, who loves all of life, go all of a sudden? Why are you letting someone's opinions and judgments ruin your day?* It made me blush a bit with embarrassment. I realized I had more healing work to do, and I consciously set about doing it by practicing my forgiveness prayer. I brought the individual to mind and said,

"(Name) _____, that which took place between us is finished now; it is over. I fully and freely forgive you, and I set you free. As I set you free, I release myself from any unhealthy attachments or feelings I still harbor toward you or the incident that caused me so much pain. I wish you all good things. I am free; you are free. Thank You, God."

I said this prayer until I could do it without clenching my teeth. Gradually, my peace returned, the sun came back out, and I went back to having an enjoyable day instead of reliving a hurtful moment from my past.

I am amused at how Spirit works if I am open to hearing Its voice. In the midst of my inner temper tantrum, the voice of reason spoke to me—not with an answer but with the question about why I was letting someone steal my peace. Within a brief time, I was laughing at myself and feeling suitably humbled. I remembered that I had a choice, so I consciously blessed the person who triggered my automatic irritation and then I forgave him and myself for falling asleep so quickly. I was reminded of a bumper sticker that reads, "It is easy to be an angel when no one is ruffling your feathers."

Who is ruffling your feathers? Be an angel—forgive and bless them. That reminds me of another bumper sticker: "Angels can fly because they take themselves so lightly."

March 2009

"We are not held back by the love we didn't receive in the past, but by the love we are not extending in the present."

Marianne Williamson

Karma: It's Never about "Them"—Dammit!

"Out beyond the ideas of right doing and wrong doing, there is a field. I will meet you there."

Rumi

What goes around comes around. How many times have we heard that? One week I had two very different demonstrations of how true that cliché can be.

On Wednesday of that week, I picked up my mail and began to sort through it. I noticed a plain white envelope with a handwritten address with a Tacoma, Washington, postmark. Tacoma is where Faith and I served as senior ministers in our first full-time Unity Ministry over twenty years ago. Our years there, under the shadow of majestic Mount Rainier, were among our most fulfilling and enjoyable. We learned great lessons and made lifelong friends.

I opened the envelope and saw what appeared to be a typewritten anonymous note on plain white paper. My first thought was, *Oh, no, an anonymous hate letter.* (Usually the most critical letters are sent anonymously.) However, when I fully opened the letter, a twenty-dollar bill fluttered onto my desk top. The letter read,

Dear Rev. Michael,

Once upon a time you gave me some assistance. I'm sending the enclosed love offering in thanks. Many thanks!

Sincerely, an Anonymous Benefactor

I cannot tell you how it warmed my heart to think something that I said or did for a person *once upon a time* was still remembered enough that they would think to gift me with twenty bucks, twenty years later. I sat there for a few moments with a grateful heart.

The other experience had quite the opposite effect on me. I received a call from a person with whom I have never had a positive relationship. After my brief communication with her, I hung up feeling depleted, agitated, angry, and toxic. We have very different values and ethics. I have to admit I have been judgmental of her from our first hello many years ago, and my thoughts of her have not always been of a positive nature. I'm sure she feels the same about me, and yet we seem to keep getting thrown together from time to time. I wonder why? Hmm...

My favorite spiritual teacher, Rabbi Raphael Levine, shared an old Jewish proverb that went something like this, "The pit you dig for another, you yourself will fall into; the blessings you confer upon another always return to crown your head."

There you have it. I was experiencing both realities based on the energy of actions of twenty or more years ago. One returned to bless me and the other to curse me or at least to remind me of the healing work I need and want to do.

Every moment each one of us sends out energy that will return in kind at some point in our lives. We are each a radiating center of positive or negative energy which ripples out to enhance or diminish our life experiences and those of others as well. Yes, we are each that powerful, and that knowledge should humble us and wake us up.

What kind of energy are you sending out today that will return to you as sure as night follows day? This is an important question to ponder. If you are unhappy with the state of your relationships and life experiences today, the only way to change them is to start radiating new positive energy into the world from this day forward.

What would you like to see come around in your future? If you are still "crucifying" someone in your mind, is this what you want to experience in the future? No one is worth that.

After I hung up from my interaction with my "adversary," I asked myself that question and decided to change the energy I was radiating right then and there. I stilled my mind and emotions as best I could and viewed her with the eyes of compassion. I wished for her a deep healing so she could finally live the life I know she desires and deserves. The moment I shifted out of judgment and into compassion and blessing, I could feel the toxic buildup begin to diminish in me, and my heart opened. What I wish for her is what I wish for myself: healing, joy, satisfaction, a sense of well-being, and self-acceptance.

The hard and wonderful truth is this: it is never about them. They merely serve as mirrors of what needs healing in our own lives. We can never control what another sends out; we can only choose what we send out. And that is what determines our quality of life and peace of mind.

August 2008

"To sit in judgment of those you perceive to be wrong or imperfect is to be one more person who is part of judgment, evil, or imperfection."

Dr. Wayne Dyer

Rewriting Our Stories

"The greatest discovery of my generation is that a human being can alter his life by altering his attitudes."
William James

Some time ago, a man came to see me seeking guidance on why he could not connect with women, among other things. He was suffering from depression. At each of our sessions he retold the same story, almost word for word, about how painful his divorce was and how he wondered whether he could ever trust a woman again. I asked him how long he had been divorced; seven years was the answer. I pointed out that each time he told the story, he was rehearsing being hurt, lonely, angry, and depressed. No wonder no one wanted to be with him. He was living out the traumatic drama despite the pain, and he had slipped into an excruciating rut no healthy woman wanted to climb into. I reminded him of the words of The Buddha, "The mind is everything. What we think we become." Unity's co-founder, Charles Fillmore, said it this way, "Thoughts held in mind produce after their kind."

Our stories either expand us or keep us small and contracted; so, what are the limiting stories you have continually told about yourself, family history, intelligence, bodies, sex, relationships, work, God, the world? Are these stories productive? Do they have positive endings, or are they ones that keep you small, angry, sad, and feeling victimized? If so, why are you still entertaining them? What is your payoff? Will these predominant life stories get you where you say you want to be?

These are important questions to ponder. I decided it was time to retire some of the old stories I have told about myself and events in my life that no longer serve me. One of my stories was I would die young because that is what happened to my dad, my mom, my wife, and her whole family. For a long time, I pretty much accepted this as my most likely scenario and unconsciously did things that would ensure the fulfillment of that deadly story. Well, *I decided* I don't like that story anymore, and on my birthday one year I started changing it. I decided the next twenty years of my life would be the most positive, productive, passionate, and prosperous years for me thus far. And after that? Who knows? How will this happen? I have no idea yet, but changing my deadly story is a very good place to begin. I fully intend to spend more quality time on this side of the dirt.

Overall, I have had a very satisfying life so far, even with more than a few major "speed bumps" along the way, and I want it to continue for at least another twenty years. So here is the question I pose to you: do you care more about retelling and reliving your past-life story than you do about creating and living a different future? All the stories you tell about yourself impact every decision you make. If you keep telling the same old story, you will keep getting the same old life, and you will always find plenty of evidence to support your well-rehearsed drama.

The only way you can recognize yourself, and your life, is through the stories you believe and tell about yourself. Many of our self-limiting stories are full of faulty assumptions and half-truths that keep us stuck in unhealthy and unsatisfying situations. Are you ready to write a new life story? I am.

That's my new story, and I'm stickin' to it!

January 2011

"Change your life today. Don't gamble on the future, act now, without delay."

Simone de Beauvoir

Prayer

"In prayer, a change of perspective takes place. The narrowness of our vision gives way to the largeness of Love's out-pouring generosity. True prayer, therefore, is essentially simple: the willingness to let go, to be transformed, to be open to receive."

Father Joe Mannath, SD

One of the many things I admired most about Faith was her deep spirituality and discipline. One night after our private Torah class at the home of our teacher, Rabbi Raphael Levine, Faith stopped him as he was showing us to the door and said, "Rabbi, tell me about your prayer life." Rabbi got this mischievous twinkle in his eyes, and he answered, "Oh, Faith, I never pray to God anymore!" Faith's jaw dropped. I could see the confusion and a bit of disappointment on her face. After he let it sink in, he repeated, "No, I never pray to God anymore. I've finally learned to just agree with God. I just say, 'Yes, God.' Goodnight, my friends." We stepped out the door and spent the rest of the evening discussing the nuances of what he had just taught us.

Prayer has been on many people's minds lately, or so it would seem, judging from the number of questions I have been receiving. One particularly frustrated man said, "I think prayer is a bunch of wishful thinking. Few of my prayers are ever answered the way I asked, so I've stopped praying. Every time I pray for something and it doesn't happen, I feel let down by God or even foolish. It has become an exercise in frustration and disappointment." If we were honest, many of us would have to admit we agree with his sentiments at one time or another. We've probably all tried the "supernatural lobbying" method of prayer.

Many people have asked if it is okay to pray for things or specific outcomes, such as healing from a disease or for some situation to be resolved in their favor. It is only human to want to pray in that way. After all, Jesus did it twice that we know of toward the end of his life. On those occasions he specifically asked that he not have to face his painful suffering and fate, and he begged Abba (God) for release (John 12:27 and Matthew 26:36–40). He then surrendered his human need with, "Not my will, but Thy will be done," and he found the strength and faith to move forward into his destiny. It did not change the outcome, but it changed the way he faced life and death.

The human part of us wants specific outcomes that please or comfort us. Sometimes our will is not in the best interest of the "Higher Way," but we still have to honor the human side of our nature. I find it helpful to ask myself the question, "Will the fulfillment of my desires cause harm to another?" If my answer is no, I will state something like this, "Loving Presence, this is the best outcome I can see now, but I trust in Your wisdom to bring about the perfect out-working for the good of all concerned. This, God, or something better."

For quite some time, I have found I rarely ask God for anything other than a greater sense of spiritual presence in my life or to experience and express a divine quality such as big love, compassion, patience, or courage. My waking prayer now is, "Thank You, God, for this most amazing new day. I am here by Divine Appointment. I am Yours to use as You will. How may I serve You today?" Perhaps this is another way of stating Rabbi's much shorter prayer, "Yes, God!"

Today you will have many opportunities to serve God, such as showing small kindnesses, refraining from gossip or complaining, or even making a healthy choice for your well-being. May you discover the power of "Yes, God!" and see how it changes you.

April 2007

"I prayed for twenty years but got nowhere until I prayed with my legs."

Frederick Douglas

Finding Your Way in Life
Being Inspired by Our Doubts

"Deep doubts, deep wisdom; small doubts, small wisdom."
Chinese proverb

A few people have expressed surprise that I occasionally entertain doubts about the nature of God, faith, or the real meaning of life, death, purpose, and so on. I think sometimes we believe that people who are called to ministry have more faith than the "average" person. I know I used to think so. Actually, I have found just the opposite to be true. Many of the people I have most admired are the ones who were riddled with doubt and moved forward in their spiritual search anyway. A case in point is the recent revelation that Mother Teresa wrestled with doubt practically her whole life, and yet her life of compassionate service touched us all. My mentor and friend, Rabbi Levine, confessed to me that he had an ongoing struggle with doubts his whole life, out of which came a desire to know the Heart of God. Another radical Rabbi, Jesus of Nazareth, certainly felt fear and doubt on numerous well-documented occasions: "My God, my God, why have you abandoned me?" None of us is exempt.

In many cases it is our doubts that fuel the search to know God more and call us to ministry, hoping to find answers. That was certainly the case for me. The truth is doubt is not a bad thing at all. We all have doubts. As a matter of fact, there is no such thing as faith without doubt. They are two sides of the same coin. You cannot have one without the other. Faith is not faith unless it is tested against doubt.

Every major accomplishment in my life started out as a major doubt or fear that I wasn't capable enough. It may have been the same for you. For instance, I was painfully shy as a child. I could not talk in front of a class or group. My voice simply would not work. In second grade, a teacher kept slapping the back of my legs with a pointer, trying to get me to read out loud. I wanted to, but I just couldn't. Then ten years later I had the outlandish dream to become a broadcaster. I had to encounter my doubts on a daily basis as I enrolled in speech classes, drama, and oral interpretation. I put my faith in my "vision" and took one shaky step at a time until finally my knees eventually stopped knocking, and I became a radio and TV personality, narrator, and speech coach. The words of the great New Thought teacher Emmett Fox certainly applied to me, "Do it trembling if you must, but you must do it!"

I also had serious doubts about my ability to be fully present in a committed relationship until I met Faith, and my desire to be with her for the rest of my life motivated me to face those fears and doubts. Faith and I both had major doubts about leaving the security of our careers and the comfortable lifestyle we enjoyed to go to seminary for three years and still meet our parental and financial obligations. For over twenty-three years, we had the most amazing life as ministers together despite our doubts that we were worthy or capable.

Doubts not faced lead to inertia or paralysis. Doubts faced lead to stronger faith. Doubt drives us deeper into the question beyond the obvious. The great C.S. Lewis wrote:

"If ours is a faith examined, we should be unafraid to doubt. If doubt is eventually justified, we were believing what clearly was not worth believing. But, if doubt is answered, our faith has grown stronger. It knows God more certainly, and it can enjoy God more deeply."

Our faith grows stronger as we question the easy, popular, or comfortable answers. Doubt can have a very positive effect in that it keeps us open to new insights and possibilities, which can lead to major breakthroughs in wisdom and understanding.

November 2007

"Focus more on your dream than your doubt, and the dream will take care of itself. You may be surprised at how easily this can happen. Your doubts are not as powerful as your desires unless you make them so."

Marcia Wieder

Practicing the Presence

"Make your work a prayer of gratitude."
Michael Moran

Over the years, one of the most frequent requests I hear is to help people get clarity on how to get more meaning out of their jobs or chosen career paths. It usually comes out something like, "I want to do something that matters. I want to find a job that has meaning. I want to work in a spiritual place helping people. I want to make a difference."

The truth is no job has any more meaning or purpose other than what we assign to it, and the truth is God is equally present in all jobs. I have known teachers, counselors, ministers, and medical professionals who are unhappy with their professions. I have also known people performing what appear to be routine and mundane jobs who are happy and fulfilled doing common tasks. The difference is they have discovered how to mindfully bring meaning to whatever they do by making it a spiritual practice.

In seventeenth-century France, there was a simple Carmelite monk named Brother Lawrence. Because he lacked education, he was not allowed to become a priest, and he was assigned the most undesirable and humble jobs in the monastery. Some of the other brothers and priests looked down on him and mocked his menial role. While the priests went about their "holy" and important business, Brother Lawrence decided to bring a sense of the sacred to every job he was assigned. He approached each simple or dirty task as an act of love.

For him the issue was not the worldly status of the assignment—it was the motivation behind it. He said, "It is not needful that we should have great things to do...we can do little things for the love of God. I can turn the cake I am frying for the love of God. I can pick up straw from the ground for the love of God." Brother Lawrence understood the holiness that is available in performing the common business of each moment. He called it "Practicing the Presence of God," and he saw his lowly workplace as his classroom. He admitted it was not always easy, but he persisted in his practice. He looked for God in every moment and in every face. His work became an act of worship. Afterward, he said, "I rise happier than a king."

No one remembers the names of the educated "holy ones" who lived at the monastery at that time, but humble Brother Lawrence is still revered to this day for the love, joy, and dedication he brought to the most routine and mundane of jobs. He found a way to honor his God right where he was, doing what was in front of him by making his work a prayer.

Every September we celebrate Labor Day, a time we have set aside to honor the American workers and the fruits of their labor. The average American worker puts in eight hours a day and another hour commuting to and from the workplace. That is nine hours! Nine hours of getting paid to Practice the Presence of God in your own workplace and to be a blessing to all who work with you. Make your work a prayer of gratitude.

"If a man is called to be a street sweeper, he should sweep streets even as Michelangelo painted, or Beethoven composed music, or Shakespeare wrote poetry. He should sweep streets so well that all the hosts of heaven and earth would pause and say, now here lived a great street sweeper who did his job well."

Rev. Dr. Martin Luther King, Jr.

Teachers in Our Lives

"Great minds have purpose, small minds have wishes. "
Washington Irving

At Spiritual Life Center, we are blessed with friendships with leaders of many spiritual faiths. One Sunday, our favorite Buddhist monk from Sri Lanka, Bhante Wimala, visited and shared his stories and wisdom with us. Bhante travels the world doing good works on behalf of the less fortunate. He is skilled in the art of connecting people and resources and making sure the goods and services get to those in need. His world is full of the worst poverty imaginable, violence, degradation, and corruption, and yet he manages to keep centered to the core of his being, which is always at peace.

I love Bhante's peaceful nature, but I most admire his humanness. As we talked, he shared his own pain and grief over the loss of his beloved mother and sister, and the murder of one of his closest associates at the hands of the Tamil Tigers in Sri Lanka. He shared how frustrating and difficult it is to not lose sight of the inherent goodness in people when you are faced with violence, graft, and corruption as you try to do good works for those who are suffering.

His sharing reminded me of a story about Mahatma Gandhi, who was facing tremendous inner struggles over the greed and corruption of some officials. When asked how he kept his faith in humankind, Gandhi said, "Humanity is an ocean. If a few drops are dirty, the whole ocean does not become dirty." Too often, we put all of our attention on the few dirty drops and give them way too much power.

The next day, I went to a friend's home to have a simple lunch of rice, steamed green vegetables, and ginger tea with Bhante. It was a wonderful lunch with just the two of us sharing about life and our purpose for being. We talked about how life doesn't always go according to our best laid plans and noblest of intentions. And yet we must adjust to life, continue to journey within, ask for guidance, listen with our hearts, and then, and only then, make our plans, and reset our noble intentions.

It is important to stay grounded in the *now* moment and not try to keep clinging to the pleasures or disappointments of a long-gone past or grasping for an uncertain future. It is only in this moment that we exist and can experience true peace and wholeness. We are each called upon to do what is before us now with mindfulness and excellence. St. Francis of Assisi was hoeing in his garden when he was asked what he would do if he were to suddenly learn he would die before sunset that day. He replied, "I would continue hoeing my garden."

What is before you now? We are all blessed with many great teachers to help us to remember to be fully present with others, to help them feel valued, to refrain from unnecessary criticism or judgment of others, to maintain a cheerful countenance, to be mindful of the task before us now, and to do all we can to be of service to others. Pretty basic stuff, but it is what matters in the end. As St. Theresa of Lisieux reminds us, "Every small task of every day is part of the total harmony of the universe."

February 2007

"Energy creates energy. It is by spending oneself that one becomes rich."

Sarah Bernhardt

The All-ness of Life

"We are never as vulnerable as when we trust someone—but paradoxically, if we cannot trust neither can we find true love or joy."
Walter Anderson

In September of 2008, I visited a dear friend from my radio days in Spokane, Washington. Her name was Stella, and she had only about three weeks left to live. Her daughter had called to tell me of her mother's condition and that Stella wanted me to conduct her Celebration of Life service when the time came. I told her I was going to be in Spokane a few days later, so Stella and I could plan it together. It was wonderful to see her and reconnect after all these years.

Stella and I talked about dying, and she was prepared and at peace, even though the news was sudden and unexpected. She said the only regret she had was she hadn't trusted enough to truly surrender to relationships in her life. Next time, she said she was going to go full tilt! I think the nurses thought we were crazy when they heard loud laughter coming from her room. Here she was, just weeks away from her next great soul adventure, and we were teasing each other and laughing. They were probably thinking, *what kind of minister is that!?* I shared a Woody Allen quote she said summed up her sentiments exactly, "I'm not afraid to die; I just don't want to be there when it happens." Stella roared at that one.

I was reminded of the time my sister, Patti, and I were sitting on our mother's bed as she was getting close to death. We were reminiscing about our time together and alternating between tears and uproarious laughter. My mom said to us in her weakened voice, "Isn't this the best? I am dying, and my kids are laughing." That's how I want to leave this life.

I am always in awe in the presence of births and deaths. They are such holy moments. We grieve the one and celebrate the other, and yet they are two aspects of the same state. The infant must die to the only universe it has ever known and physically separate from its source in order to be born into a more expansive existence. When we die, it is much the same—we must die to this world and release every earthly attachment in order to move on to the next phase. I am not certain what happens next; it is great mystery, but I totally trust the process. Here is one of the best mental images I have ever read of the dying process. It is by Henry Van Dyke.

> I am standing upon the seashore.
> A ship at my side spreads her white sails to the morning breeze and starts for the blue ocean.
> She is an object of beauty and strength.
> I stand and watch her until at length she hangs like a speck of white cloud just where the sea and sky come to mingle with each other.
> Then, someone at my side says, "There, she is gone!"

"Gone where?"

Gone from my sight. That is all.

She is just as large in mast and hull and spar as she was when she left my side and she is just as able to bear her load of living freight to her destined port.

Her diminished size is in me, not in her.

And just at the moment when someone at my side says, "There, she is gone!"

There are other eyes watching her coming, and other voices ready to take up the glad shout, "Here she comes!"

And that is dying.

Days after Stella's passing, Sophia Faith Moran was born into the world. She is the child of Faith's and my son Talor and daughter in-law Melisse. She is magnificent! Every baby is the perfect baby to its parents and grandparents, but Sophia Faith is extra special to me because she was conceived in January during the final weeks of her Grandma Faith's life. I could feel Faith's presence as I held little Sophia for the first time. This has been an amazing year of endings and beginnings. Wow…what a year. Talk about the all-ness of life!

September 2008

"I don't believe people are looking for the meaning of life as much as they are looking for the experience of being alive."

Joseph Campbell

Trusting Divine Order

"Once you finally make a decision, the Universe conspires to make it happen."
Ralph Waldo Emerson

On August 10, 2009, Reverend Christine Bouten, Senior Minister of Operations, and I signed the purchase papers on the new home for the Spiritual Life Center's (SLC) offices, classrooms, chapel, and bookstore. To use Christine's words, it was a surreal experience.

Together, over the past eight years, we have looked at approximately one hundred properties and have made offers on at least twenty-five of them. Each time the offer was accepted, for some unexpected reason it was pulled off the table at the last minute. It was frustrating and at times disheartening for everyone, especially the ministers and building-search teams who had put so much time and energy into the process only to come up empty-handed time and again. It seemed we were not intended to have our own place.

Now that we have secured a home of our own, I look back at some of the places we came so close to acquiring, and I enthusiastically echo the words of the country song by Garth Brooks, "Thank God for unanswered prayers!" None of us could have foreseen the dramatic changes that were ahead of us, such as the illness and death of Reverend Faith Moran and the dramatic downturn of the world's economy. Both events had severely impacted our income for a period of time. We would have been in a real mess if any of those deals had gone through. Everything was in Divine Order, even when it seemed otherwise.

That is an important point to remember. Each attempt we made to buy a new home for SLC taught us some important lessons and tested our faith and resolve. Nothing was wasted even when the deals fell through. We learned to live with the disappointment of unmet expectations and not give in to cynicism and hopelessness. At each seeming dead-end, we learned to step back, breathe, pray for more guidance, practice forgiveness and patience, and then begin again. Our continual prayer was, "Thank You, God, for this or something better."

Perhaps the greatest of all lessons was one of non-attachment. I think that is why Rev. Christine and I both felt a sort of *surrealism* at the time of final signing. We had prayed that prayer so many times that we approached the purchase with a sort of detached acceptance of whatever served the greater good. We left the title company feeling nothing but gratitude and a deep knowing that this was the right next step for Spiritual Life Center.

I truly believe all things happen for a reason. That doesn't mean we don't get hurt or disappointed or even disillusioned when things don't go according to our individual wishes, but at least at our core we can know everything is in Divine Order all the time. Every action has a corresponding reaction, and every choice we make has consequences. How we choose to move forward is up to us. That is free will.

As I was preparing to move my office this week and clearing out twelve years of accumulated files, I came across something that spoke to me. This is by an unknown author, and it is dedicated to all those who have made and will make a difference in our lives.

Things Happen for a Reason

"Sometimes people come into your life and you know right away that they were meant to be there; to serve some sort of a purpose, teach you a lesson or help figure out who you are or want to become. You never know who these people may be, but when you lock eyes with them, you know that very moment they will affect your life in some profound ways. And sometimes things happen to you that may seem horrible, painful and unfair, but in reflection you realize that without overcoming these obstacles you would have never realized your full potential, strength or will power.

"Everything happens for a reason. Nothing happens by chance, or by means of good luck, illness, injury, love or lost moments of true greatness and sheer stupidity. All occur and will test the limits of your soul. Without these small tests, life would be like a smoothly paved, straight, flat road to nowhere—safe and comfortable, but dull and utterly pointless.

"The people you meet along the way affect your life. The successes and downfalls you experience can create who you are, and the bad experiences can be learned from. In fact they are probably the most poignant and important ones. If someone hurts you, betrays you, or breaks your heart, forgive them because they have helped you learn about trust and the importance of being cautious to whom you open your heart.

"If someone loves you, love them back unconditionally, not only because they love you, but because they are teaching you to love, and open your heart and eyes to the little things. Make every day count, appreciate every moment and take from it everything that you possibly can, for you may never be able to experience it again.

"Let yourself fall in love, risk, break free, and set your sights high. Hold your head up, because you have every right to. Remind yourself that you are a great individual and believe in yourself, for if you don't, no one else will believe in you. Create your own life, and then go out and live it."

Amen to that!

August 2009

"Attachment is the great fabricator of illusions; reality can be attained only by someone who is detached."

Simone Weil

Stretching Our Minds

"One's mind, once stretched by a new idea, never regains its original dimensions."
Oliver Wendell Holmes

Community

"Promise a lot, but give more."
Anthony De'Angelo

Many years ago, Faith and I attended a ministers' conference featuring Bishop John Shelby Spong as the keynote speaker. We had been fans and students of his for many years. Bishop Spong asked the six hundred or so ministers a question that was met with an uneasy silence. He asked, "If your church burned to the ground tonight—ceased to exist—tomorrow would anybody outside of your own congregation even know it was gone or had ever been there? If your answer is no, or you're unsure, then why in the heck are you there in the first place?"

Faith and I practically jumped out of our seats. We had observed how many churches focus only on themselves and pay little heed to people outside of their own congregation. Over the years, we had battled with church boards of trustees over becoming more involved in meeting the genuine needs of the less fortunate among us, as we also minister to members of our immediate spiritual family. Bishop Spong's well-aimed question stirred up a resolve in us, and we excitedly talked about what it would mean to be an intentional force for good in the city or town in which we served, as well as the greater world community. We vowed the next time we found ourselves leading another church, we would insist it be a community dedicated to hands-on service and tithing to the greater community. Service and giving became our core values. That opportunity presented itself a year later in 1998, when we pioneered Spiritual Life Center (SLC) in Sacramento, California.

The founding board was enthusiastic about being a spiritual community dedicated to service and financially supporting the nonprofit organizations that specialize in housing, clothing, feeding, educating, and protecting our less fortunate brothers and sisters. We wanted, as two of our earliest SLC goals, to build the first Interfaith Habitat for Humanity home and to give away one million dollars from tithes and special gifts within the first decade of service. Within the first several years, we financed and built the Habitat House with the help of Muslims, Sihks, Hindus, Buddhists, and Christians, and we refurbished a home for a wonderful elderly woman in Oak Park, California. It took us longer than expected to gift the million dollars, but we reached that goal near the end of our eleventh year.

Over the years, people have asked me where our gifts and tithes go. The vast majority of the money (80 percent) is designated for service agencies and programs in the Sacramento region. Our tithing committee mindfully chooses which agencies are in most need, and the board approves the allocation of funds each month. These gifts have helped ease the suffering and improve the quality of life for hundreds of thousands of people over the years. We also support our parent organizations such as Unity School, The Association of Unity Churches, Silent Unity, and The Association for Global New Thought, and other spiritual organizations working to improve the spiritual lives of millions.

When natural disasters occur, such as earthquakes in Iran, tsunamis in Sri Lanka, and hurricanes in the gulf region of the United States, we take up special offerings and give 100 percent of those gifts, and a portion of the SLC tithe, to designated relief organizations. We have also purchased solar flashlights and cookers for African villages that have no power and school supplies for a girls' school in war-torn Afghanistan.

Of all the things I have been able to oversee in almost twenty-five years of ministry, this is the accomplishment of which I am most satisfied and "proud." We have been faithful to the spiritual principle of giving and receiving without fail during high times and low times. Pride is one of the seven deadly sins, but I have to admit when a group of young ministers asked me what has been my "peak" ministerial experience so far, I told them it is that we were approaching the million-dollar giving amount, and their eyes widened as they exclaimed, "Seriously? Wow!" Forgive me, but I felt pride. Pride that our community walks its talk. Pride that even as we struggled financially, we never failed in our mission to serve those struggling even more. Pride that the individuals of the SLC congregation made it all possible. Pride that if SLC ceased to exist tomorrow, it would not go unnoticed.

Thanks a million to all who gave—thank you for your trust and your generous hearts. *Thanks a million* to over four hundred organizations in Sacramento that serve so faithfully to ease suffering and to generate hope. Together we have made a positive difference in our community and the greater world community.

June 2010

"If you don't know where you are going, then any road will get you there."

Lewis Carroll

As of September 2013, Spiritual Life Center has donated more than $1,250,000 to other nonprofit organizations, primarily in the Sacramento area.

True Marriage

"Be who you are, and say what you feel, because those who mind don't matter, and those who matter don't mind."

Dr. Seuss

Several years ago, Aubrey, a young woman in our teen group, asked to interview me for a paper she was writing on how different spiritual traditions and religions view marriage, specifically same-sex marriage.

Her first question was: "Do you believe in marriage? Why or why not?"

Yes, I do believe in marriage but not as it is currently defined in the *Merriam-Webster Dictionary*. The dictionary defines marriage as, "The state of being united to a person of the opposite sex as husband and wife in a consensual and contractual relationship recognized by law." Notice there is no mention of love or caring in this definition.

For me, true marriage is much more than a legal arrangement uniting two adults in a legal contractual relationship. That sounds more like a civil contract or domestic partnership where two people are legally bound together. They must agree to certain conditions and responsibilities which provide a legal safety net that protects the couple and holds them accountable. I believe everyone who chooses to live together as committed partners would be wise to enter into a civil union, but I would not call that a marriage. As defined by most states today, a marriage is legal once the couple, and an officiate, sign the license, which then automatically grants over fifteen hundred federal and state rights and responsibilities to the man and woman.

The second question was, "Do you think same-sex marriage should be legal? Why or why not?"

Times and minds are changing, and I, for one, definitely support same-gender marriage. Why? Marriage to me is a sacred spiritual covenant uniting two souls already in harmony with one another. It is between two people who deeply love and care for one another and choose to make a public declaration of their love and commitment. This sacred ceremony is about the love and commitment of these two consenting adults, not their gender.

As a Unity minister, I believe when two people stand together and publicly declare their love for one another and their intention to build a committed life together, they should be celebrated and affirmed. The institution of marriage in the United States is not going to be harmed by allowing two committed, loving people their equal and moral rights. If you were to check the number of marriage licenses granted in most counties per year against the number of divorces granted, you would find the numbers very close indeed. I believe my gay and lesbian friends can do at least as well as that. True love is rare enough and deserves to be treasured and honored regardless of gender.

Some dissenters of same-sex marriage use the Judeo-Christian Bible as the literal guide for maintaining the status quo. I remind us that the same Bible has been liberally quoted to justify and uphold many evils such as slavery, subjugation of women and minorities, and polygamy (Solomon had over six hundred wives and hundreds of concubines). It goes on to deny crippled or blind people, dwarves, people with blemishes, flat noses (seriously), and men with crushed "stones" access to houses of worship and full membership into the religious community. I could go on and on, but you get the picture. You have to be very careful when you use the Bible, or any scripture, as the literal word of God, especially when you are trying to justify your own prejudice—it can backfire on you.

The God of my understanding loves all people and welcomes men and women, gay or straight, who wish to enter into a lifelong covenant of loving, caring for, and supporting one another on life's journey. Some of my proudest moments as a minister came when there was a brief window of opportunity in California to perform legally sanctioned marriages for same-gender couples. I struggled to hold back tears of joy the first time I declared, "It is under the authority of the State of California and in the name of The Spirit of Love, which seals every true marriage, I now pronounce you legally wed, partners for life!" Holy marriage is about committed love, not gender.

I am pretty sure I gave Aubrey more than she needed, but I am grateful that her questions allowed me to further examine my beliefs concerning this important issue of our time.

March 2010

"Where ignorance is the master, there is no possibility for real peace."

The Dalai Lama

What Does a Cult Look Like, Really?

"I wonder if other dogs think poodles are members of some weird religious cult?"
Rita Rudner

Spiritual Life Center (SLC), the church that Faith and I started in Sacramento, is primarily an Interfaith Community based on Unity teachings. It was always exciting when new people, especially young families, were guided to visit and check us out. I always enjoyed experiencing SLC through the eyes of someone who was hearing and connecting with the message of inclusiveness, Unity, and Oneness for the first time.

I remember well my early days in Unity when I would try to hide my tears of relief and gratitude each Sunday as we held hands and sang the "Peace Song." I felt like an orphaned child who suddenly discovered he was part of a much larger family who looked, thought, and felt the same way. Before that, I felt all alone with my beliefs. It was like a spiritual homecoming.

Inevitably, many of those new to Unity and SLC were confronted by family and friends who warned them about getting involved with this Unity-Interfaith cult. Their loved ones sincerely feared for their souls' salvation and tried to warn them, shame them, or scare them back onto the "true path." This caused pain and confusion to those new to SLC who were so filled with joy at their new discovery. They would often seek me out to express their irritation and concerns and to find reassurance that SLC was not leading them down the "wrong and narrow path."

I encouraged them to decide for themselves whether the community they had experienced at SLC fit these generally accepted characteristics of a religious cult.

(1) A religious cult is likely centered on a leader or organization that claims special spiritual knowledge or messiah-like qualities.

(2) The group members view themselves as spiritually superior and see their way as the only way. They denounce anyone who believes otherwise.

(3) They often promote an "us versus them" mentality, which causes division in the larger society.

(4) Members use fear, shame, shunning, threats of eternal damnation, and other forms of coercion against those who stray.

(5) A cult requires, or expects, its followers to actively recruit and convert non-believers.

(6) Free thinking or inquiry is discouraged and often forbidden.

As far as I could see, Unity, New Thought, and SLC didn't fit any of these cult characteristics. We actually seemed to be the antithesis of all six.

Admittedly, Unity, New Thought, and SLC are not for everyone, especially those seeking more structure and definitive answers to life's toughest questions. We teach the answers to these valuable questions are not found outside of us but inside of us. At SLC, we seek to provide spiritual tools and techniques to help discern the voice of God and discover the Divine Wisdom within each of us.

If SLC is a cult then it is one that actively encourages freedom of thought, the value and worth of diverse spiritual practices, kindness, compassion, a God who loves all equally, and the Oneness of all life. If Unity and Spiritual Life Center are cults then sign me up!

"All differences in this world are of degree, and not of kind, because oneness is the secret of everything."

Vivekananda

New Thought Guilt

Have you ever gone to a New Thought church service, meeting, or seminar and left feeling guilty or unworthy with your self-esteem battered and bruised? If so, it was probably because you heard the minister or leader say something like, "You are responsible for everything in your life, so why did you choose to get cancer, or go bankrupt, break your leg, cross paths with that wacko, or...?" You get the picture?

A woman I know was having difficulty with her vision, and her ophthalmologist told her she would certainly go blind without surgery to correct the problem. The prospect of going blind was understandably frightening to her. One of her well-meaning friends asked her, "What are you refusing to see in your life that you have manifested this?" Suddenly she felt judged and guilty of turning a blind eye toward some unpleasantness she had created. She was told that as soon as she dealt with that "unseen" issue, her sight would return to normal. Her friend advised her to cancel her surgery and follow a non-medical alternative of meditation, a special restricted diet, and spiritual cleansing. She asked me if I thought she should follow her friend's advice and cancel the surgery. I said, "It all sounds good *except* the 'cancel the surgery' part." I am a firm believer in what I call "meditate and medicate." I teach that God is everywhere fully present, which means Spirit works through prayers and doctors, medical procedures, and medications as well. Turn within and go where God directs.

Over the years, I have spoken with more than a few people who have received some potentially catastrophic news concerning their own health or that of a loved one. Others have lost jobs, homes, or relationships and been catapulted into a lonely, frightening, and unfamiliar world. A common question is, "Why is this happening to me?" No matter how enlightened we like to think we may be, almost everyone I know has had that question surface at a time of trauma. It is so very human.

What concerns me is how much judgment and guilt we "New Thought folks" sometimes lay on ourselves or others when things get scary. How many of us have said that one of the reasons we abandoned mainstream religion was because of the so-called guilt trips? What we didn't realize was that we faced a whole new form of guilt that is equally as damaging to our self-esteem and quality of life—it is called New Thought Guilt. Old-time religion told us to feel guilty about almost everything that made us feel good; the New Thought version is to feel guilty about feeling less than positive, healthy, and abundant all the time!

It is so tempting to slip into the dangerous and erroneous thinking of *what did I do wrong to have created this? It's all my fault. I must not be a good person. How did I do this to myself? I must be weak. I must have screwed up in a past life! If only I had more faith, I could make this go away.* This or some version of "monkey-mind thinking" goes on and on, and we torture ourselves needlessly. (Be sure to not feel guilty if you have ever had one of those thoughts.)

It is important to examine our lives and be accountable for whatever we *may* have done that *may* have contributed to a painful or unhealthy situation. But we also need to realize sometimes "stuff" just happens. Remember, our individual conscious is constantly interacting with elements and people over whom we have little or no control at all.

I believe we truly are powerful beings, but we are not so powerful as to be responsible for every sniffle, dented car door, angry neighbor, lost job, flat tire, vicious dog, or serious diagnosis that comes our way. Our true power is in the fact that we have total control over our thoughts and attitudes in every situation. It is through the practice of well-documented New Thought spiritual methods that we learn how to create inner peace and receive clear guidance from our Divine Nature as to how to respond to life's joys and disappointments.

By using the power of affirmative prayer, meditation, creative visualize, and forgiveness, we can greatly influence desired outcomes and enhance our enjoyment of life. What is most valuable is that we learn how to establish and maintain our mind and heart at peace as we navigate life. That's what Jesus was talking about when he cautioned us not to focus on unpredictable outer conditions.

"Do not lay up for yourselves treasures on earth, where moth and rust can destroy, and thieves can break in and steal. Rather lay up for yourselves treasures in heaven—for where your treasure is, there your heart will be also." Again, focus on the inside, and the outside will take care of itself.

One of my favorite quotes that has helped me stay focused on positive outcomes during challenging times is by Unity's co-founder, Charles Fillmore, "This situation before us is pregnant with possibilities for good!" I must admit many times I have thought to myself, *Well, the good is certainly well-disguised in there!* It always helps to keep a good sense of humor.

To those who may have said you were *totally* responsible for every "itty-bitty" thing that went wrong (or right) in your life, I now charge them with metaphysical malpractice. Please instruct them to report to the Karma police and turn in their revoked metaphysical licenses.

"We have no right to ask when sorrow comes, 'Why did this happen to me?' unless we ask the same question for every moment of happiness that comes our way."

Unknown

Separation of Church and State

I am a minister who strongly believes in separation of church and state. The reason? It seems each time religion and politics climb into bed together, the offspring is always ill-conceived. If I sound a little preachy here, forgive me. Mea culpa in advance.

Once I had one of those nights when I couldn't fall back to sleep after waking up at 2:51 a.m., and I finally got up and settled in on the sofa. In an attempt to lull myself back to sleep, I channel-surfed and came across a news program that was reporting on the presidential candidates and their religious piety. Each candidate was shamelessly pandering to the religionists in the viewing audience. Quite frankly I found it creepy, and their words sent a chill up my spine. Who are these people who have the audacity to apply a religious litmus test to a politician, or anyone else, for that matter?

As I sat there listening, the words of Radical Rabbi Jesus, whom most on the panel claimed to love, honor, and obey, came to mind:

> "Beware of practicing your righteousness before men to be noticed by them; otherwise you have no reward with your Father who is in heaven. When you give to the poor do not sound trumpets before you as the hypocrites do in the synagogues, and in the streets so that they may be honored by men" (Matthew 6:1–2).

Jesus went on to warn,

> "When you pray, you are not to be like the hypocrites; for they love to stand in synagogues and on street corners so that they may be seen by men. But you, when you pray, go into your inner room and close the door and pray to your Father who is in secret, and your Father who sees what is done in secret will reward you" (Matthew 6:5–6).

Now, I do not consider myself to be a Bible scholar, but I get this. It is simple and direct. Do not make a big, showy public display or declaration of your religion. Do it quietly, privately, humbly. Most of these "righteous" inquisitors appear to be the ones who loudly proclaim, "Jesus said it, I believe it, and that settles it!" Well? He seemed crystal clear to me on this one—not much wiggle room.

Jesus also told his followers exactly how to identify a truly good person: "You will know them by their fruits" (Matthew 7:16). I know many good and spiritual people who are not in the least bit religious, and I know many so-called religious people who appear to be anything but spiritual.

When the Dalai Lama was asked about his religion, he stated, "My religion is very simple. My religion is kindness." I like that. The absolute best answer I ever heard to the "litmus test" was while sitting on an interfaith panel and someone asked the man sitting next to me if he considered himself to be a real Christian. Without hesitating, he said, "I'll tell you what. Why don't you watch me for a while and then you tell me?" Brilliant! I wish I had said that.

"Say nothing of my religion. It is known to God and myself alone. Its evidence before the world is to be sought in my life: if it has been honest and dutiful to society the religion which has regulated it cannot be a bad one."

Thomas Jefferson

Civility in Politics

"When the power of love overcomes the love of power, then the world will know peace."

Jimi Hendrix

Honorable—fair—just—sincere—honest—principled—dignified—civil—trustworthy. Are these words you would use to describe the current Congress of the United States or politicians in general? Sadly, I would not. I know there are some elected officials in all parties who personify those attributes, but the truth is, in 2011, over 89 percent of the American public rated our Congress as ineffective, inadequate, and untrustworthy. What has gone wrong? This is not a politically motivated question; it is a spiritual one that goes to the state of the soul of our nation. Who have we allowed ourselves to become as a people?

Slogans, words, signs, and political ads that even remotely encourage violence against political opponents are just dangerously wrong. That same year, nineteen citizens were gunned down in Tucson, Arizona, while attending a political meet-and-greet with their congresswoman. Thirteen were wounded, among them US Congresswoman Gabrielle Giffords; six other innocent people were killed, including one of her aides, a federal judge, and a nine-year-old girl. Our nation was shocked and outraged, and everyone seemed to be pointing the finger of blame at someone else. No one knows for sure if the gunman was directly, or even indirectly, motivated by the nasty political hate speech that is prevalent now, but we know it has to be adding to a negatively supercharged and dangerous atmosphere in our country. This has to stop.

Over the years I have expressed my distress at the rapid decline of civility in our national discourse. I find the escalating "hate speech" being used by our elected leaders on both sides of the aisle, and by the ratings-hungry media personalities who thrive on toxic discourse, reprehensible. Words have great power to inspire us, as individuals and as a nation, to greatness or reduce us to pettiness. I know from personal experience that well-chosen loving and empowering words can reach deep into a person's soul and bring them back from the depths of despair and change the whole course of one's life. When spoken by our elected leaders, in whom we place our trust, they can change the world. Read or listen to the words of Mahatmas Gandhi, John F. Kennedy, Martin Luther King, Jr., or Nelson Mandela, and you hear greatness being asked of everyone. They spoke to our higher natures. Today, our national trust has been violated by those we elected who seem to have no fidelity to truth, and we allowed it to happen.

Toxic words directed toward a person, race, culture, religion, or nation are purposefully intended to "push buttons" and elicit a corresponding emotional response. Sadly, this has become a "black art" form, and some unscrupulous officials and commentators have become masterful at it. We also share responsibility for this because each time we tune in to a so-called news program such as the ones offered on Fox News and MSNBC, we are supporting this kind of unbalanced, "snarky," and dangerous discourse. Each time one of our elected officials spews hate speech from our hallowed halls of power or on the campaign trail, and we do not express immediate outrage and demand an end to it, we are culpable as well.

For me, this is more than just a strong opinion; it is a spiritual issue that impacts the very soul of our nation. While I was in ministerial school, the Book of James really spoke to me as I was preparing to teach spiritual truths as I understood them. James was writing to the new leaders of the movement, and he was very clear how vital words are when used by those who accept and assume positions of authority. In James 3:2–6, he writes,

"We all make many mistakes, but those who control their tongues can also control themselves in every way. We can make a large horse turn by putting a small bit in its mouth. And a tiny rudder can make a huge ship turn wherever the pilot wants it to go, even when the winds are fierce. A tiny spark can set a vast forest ablaze. And the tongue is a flame of fire. So also, my brothers and sisters, the tongue is a small thing, but enormous damage it can do…it can ruin your entire life."

I believe we have a spiritual responsibility to get our nation back on track and demand an end to this hateful, toxic speech being used so freely and destructively by those who are supposed to have our nation's best interests at heart. Even if the gunman in Arizona was not influenced in the least by the political hate speech, by allowing it to continue we are creating an atmosphere that will burn us all in the end. Irrational people respond accordingly to irrational hate speech. We must put a stop to this or our national spirit will wither and die.

Since we cannot control others, let us all pledge to watch our own tongues and control the flow of energy we send forth with our words. I encourage us to stop supporting media outlets that continue to incite and divide us. Let us call, write, or somehow contact our local, state, and national lawmakers and inform them we will not tolerate this dangerous and shameful behavior any longer. I will close my well-intentioned diatribe with this passage from Proverbs 18:21, "Death and life are in the power of your tongue, and you can give life or you can give death." Let us agree to give *life!*

January 2011

"United we stand, divided we fall."

Aesop

Compassionate Living

"Compassion is the basis for all morality. "

Arthur Shopenhauer

In July 2012, the nation and world was stunned by the senseless murder of twelve innocents and wounding of fifty-eight others by a lone gunman armed with legal military assault weapons firing into a packed movie theater. The mayhem, lasting just over a minute, terrorized our nation and world. As I watched the news that morning, my mind went numb as the death toll mounted, and shocked survivors tried to make sensc of it. My heart ached for the families and friends of the victims. I kept asking the questions, "What is wrong with our society that this is becoming more commonplace? What does this say about the spiritual state of the soul of our society?" In the United States, a country I love, the "overall firearm-related death rate among U.S. children younger than fifteen years of age is nearly twelve times higher than among children in twenty-five other industrialized countries combined."[1]

How do we respond spiritually to this type of news? As you can see by my opening paragraph, my first reaction was to blame and try to figure it all out. I was angry at whoever committed this heinous crime and wanted them brought to justice. I still want justice served. Eventually my heart started to open, and what I wanted more than anything was healing for the grieving families, our nation, and, yes, even the shooter, who is obviously a tormented soul. My capacity for compassion began to expand when I saw a news video of his father, who was rushing to Colorado to be with his son. As a father, I put myself in his place, and my heart reached out to him. The more I considered the shooter's mom and dad, the more my heart opened to their unimaginable pain. Not only have the parents of the victims lost someone precious and dear to them, the parents of James Edward Holmes have lost their son, and they will forever live with the burden of knowing their child caused it all. How tragic for everyone.

Do you find yourself thinking, *he doesn't deserve any compassion— look at what he's done?* Keep in mind that compassion is different than justice. I still want justice done, but I don't have any idea what it is like inside a tormented mind where one's sense of reality is as twisted and dark as what his mind must be.

I realized how easy it is for us to feel compassion for those people we identify with and experiences we understand. We have all experienced loss of some sort, so when devastation from earthquakes, fires, accidents, or hurricanes hits communities or families, we, as a nation and as individuals, open our hearts and our wallets to the victims. We have tremendous compassion when we know what that kind of loss feels like. Most of us are blessed to not have ever experienced the torment of a twisted, dark, and unstable mind. I feel myself wanting to just "be right" and make him pay for his crime. But doesn't compassion include being willing to feel for the pain of others, even when we don't understand them?

Even though compassion is the foundation of most, if not all, of the major spiritual paths, it is often viewed as a weakness in today's world. One person wrote to me and declared that the "real" world we occupy, which is filled with nationalistic and faith-driven hate and violence, needs something much more tangible and sophisticated than "Kumbaya-like compassion" to solve its problems. Obviously many share this belief as private gun sales in Colorado and other states sky-rocketed after the Aurora massacre, but this type of response hasn't worked so far, as we are already the best-armed population in the world. According to a recent report done by the Graduate Institute of International and Development Studies in Geneva, the United States leads the world in private gun ownership, with Serbia a distant second. If more firepower were truly the answer to ensure the peace, wouldn't we already be the most peaceful nation in the world?

Even the mention of the word *gun* creates polarization on each side of the gun-control issue. Perhaps with more compassion toward issues we do not understand, we could learn how to open meaningful conversations toward a resolution that protects the rights of gun owners but also provides protection from emotionally unstable people with six thousand rounds of ammunition easily available to them.

Taking it beyond this one issue, if we are ever to start a dialogue toward fixing the things upon which both sides of the aisle of our political system actually agree—fixing the infrastructure, for instance—we need to allow compassion to open our hearts, our minds, and our ears to listen and try to understand "the other side." I know, for the life of me, sometimes I cannot understand why followers of the other political party feel and believe the way they do, and I know they feel the same way about the party I believe in. We must find some common ground and areas where we can agree with one another—compassion may be a starting point. We must ask ourselves, "How is the current polarization working for us?"

Perhaps it is time we give compassion a genuine test. I don't pretend to know how to fully practice compassion yet, but I am willing to improve. Gandhi, King, and Mandela used it to change nations. My wife, Faith, proved to me that radical compassion is possible for all of us. Four months after we were married, her mother was murdered in her own home. Faith, of course, was devastated, and she went into a period of shock and deep mourning. One day just a week to ten days after the crime, she came out of her prayer and meditation time and called me to her, saying, "Michael, we must pray every day for the people who killed my mother. Pray with me for the healing of their souls' sickness so they never do this to anyone else." She prayed for them every day, even as she sought to bring them to justice.

Faith certainly had her moments, but overall she was the most peaceful and genuinely happy person I have ever known. In spite of the trauma she endured as a child, she still showered even her abusers with compassion. I used to think she was naïve, but now I realize she was on to the Truth. I think the Dalai Lama has it right when he says, "The emotions most disturbing our tranquility are fear and hatred. The antidote is compassion. If you want others to be happy, practice compassion. If *you* want to be happy, practice compassion."

July 2012

"The weak always resort to violence. Compassion and nonviolence are weapons of the brave."

Unknown

Easter at the Mosque

"Well done! You made the world proud."
Huffington Post reader

Early in 2012, just weeks before Easter, our most-attended Sunday service of the year, Spiritual Life Center (SLC) lost its lease with the church where we held our Sunday services each week. In April, the Sacramento Area League of Associated Muslims (SALAM) and SLC made interfaith history by doing what we have done since the very beginning of Spiritual Life Center. Our mission has always been to foster peace by bringing different faith traditions together in educational and cooperative efforts so we could learn from each other as we worked toward the common good. That was expressed so magnificently Easter Sunday as the Sacramento Area League of Associated Muslims graciously opened their home to SLC so we could conduct our most important service of the year on holy ground. When the news first broke, it was picked up by the world's largest Christian newspaper, and the comments that were generated were overwhelmingly negative and even hateful. I had expected opposition but not the volume it generated, nor the mean and "snarky" tone. I do not think that is what Jesus had in mind when he was instructing us to be loving peacemakers, extend kindness to those who are different, and to do unto others as we would have them do unto us.

Some of my friends who read the nasty comments directed at me asked if they were hurtful, and I said no. However, it did make me a little sad for those who feel they have to demean and demonize all who do not share their narrow view of God or Christianity. Being referred to as "Rev. Moron, the California whack-job" did make me laugh, though. I didn't take any of it personally because it had nothing to do with me. I am secure in my own faith and do not seek approval or agreement from others. I stopped arguing and defending my faith beliefs long ago when I decided to just endeavor to practice them, which is much more difficult but, oh, so rewarding.

The Easter services at the SALAM Mosque Complex exceeded my greatest hopes and expectations. Everything went flawlessly thanks to a collaborative effort between the SLC and SALAM volunteers working side by side. Great joy and love radiated out to everyone who attended. This was an Easter like no other.

The event went off without any protests or incidents, and the comments that have been pouring in have been overwhelmingly positive. Here is a sampling.

> "It gives me hope that we can look past our differences and focus on goodness. This story brought tears to my eyes."

"Thank you for your wonderful spirit. I am not a religious person, but I believe that all should practice what they believe. It is intelligence such as this that will eventually lead to peace."

"To use a favorite word of one of my British friends— *Brilliant!*"

"This is absolutely amazing and one of the most beautiful things I have ever read. It should be on the front page, not buried. How sad that anyone could have a problem with this. Hopefully this is only a first step in a journey of interfaith cooperation."

"Simply outstanding. Republicans and Democrats should read this and practice the lesson here...hope springs eternal."

"All I can say is *observe and learn*. This is a worthwhile lesson."

There were hundreds more positive comments, but this gives you a sense of how this significant interfaith moment was perceived by many in a deeply divided world. Thank you again to our friends at SALAM for their kindness and hospitality and for making it possible. This was an Easter we will never forget. May it be just the beginning. Hallelujah!

I will close with a line from one of my favorite Psalms (133): "Behold how pleasant and good it is when brothers and sisters dwell together in unity." Thank You, God!

April 2012

"We have lived our lives by the assumption that what was good for us would be good for the world. We have been wrong. We must change our lives so that it will be possible to live by the contrary assumption, that what is good for the world will be good for us. And that requires that we make the effort to know the world and learn what is good for it."

Wendell Berry

The Cosmic Lounge

"Some luck lies in not getting what you thought you wanted but getting what you have, which once you have got it, you may be smart enough to see it is what you would have wanted had you known."

Oliver Wendell Holmes

I was giddy with happiness and excited about seeing some old friends and acquaintances I had not been with for what seemed like eons. I had put out the call for all to assemble at a particular time and place. I was running behind, and as I rushed to get there, I could just hear them good-naturedly jeering me as I arrived fashionably late. I laughed to myself as I anticipated their jokes and kidding.

It was in a pure white, nondescript city where I found myself, but I seemed to know exactly where I was heading, as if I had been there many times before. I finally arrived at a small building with a very old-fashioned door made of tucked-and-rolled Naugahyde and a round porthole for a window. It was the kind of door you see on a cheesy, out-of-date cocktail lounge. That's exactly what it was. Above the door in bright green neon was a sign that read, *"Welcome to the Cosmic Lounge."*

I opened the door, and light flooded into the dim interior. As my eyes adjusted, I could see dust particles floating in the beam of light that illuminated the old-fashioned lounge. To my left was a bartender, who was wiping glasses behind the bar. He looked up, recognized me, smiled, and pointed. "Mike, they've been waiting for you. They're right over there." I looked to my right, and, there, sitting at a large round table, were people I had known during a very intense, confusing, often painful, and pivotal period of my life. Some I knew well, some I liked, and some I could not stand, but they were all there, laughing, joking, and animatedly talking with each other like old friends. One of them looked up and said, "Well, wouldn't ya know—here he is, finally! He calls the meeting, and naturally he shows up late." As I had anticipated, the friendly chiding began. I didn't care; I was just so thrilled they were there for this important moment.

Inherently, I knew they had traveled at great personal effort and sacrifice, but each felt it was important to be there on this particular day. I was deeply moved by this and gratefully took my place at the table as they kept asking, "Are you sure this is the day? I mean really sure? Because I've got things to do, ya know. It wasn't easy getting away." The longer we sat there talking, laughing, and waiting, the more they kept asking me if I was sure. I kept reassuring them, "Yes, this is the day. Trust me," which drew more guffaws from them. At this point I still didn't consciously know what we were actually there for, but I knew we had agreed to meet at this time and this place. For what, though?

Suddenly a bell chimed, signaling the arrival of an elevator. All talking stopped, and, in unison, we turned to look toward the

elevator. The door opened smoothly, and there stood Helene, looking dazed and a bit bewildered as she stared at the collection of
familiar people, all waiting for her arrival. At this point, I somehow
knew I had been dead, as were all the others who had come back
for this special occasion. Back from where? That I didn't know.

I stood up and walked over to her, feeling the most pure love
I have ever experienced. I wrapped my arms around her and
pulled her to me, saying, "Helene, you were magnificent! I swear
to God, you gave an Academy Award performance. You really had
me going. I loved you so deeply it frightened me; I absolutely
despised you at times, but you broke me open like no one else
could. For that I am eternally grateful. You played your part beautifully. Thank you!"

Helene replied, "Oh, Michael, I loved you so. You were perfect
for me as well. I learned so much from you. You opened me to my
spiritual nature, and I have never been the same since. You were
perfect for me."

I then said something that surprised me since I thought I had
always wanted to hear her apologize to me for abruptly leaving
the dysfunctional couple's drama we had acted out so many years
ago. I looked into her soft, beautiful eyes and said, "Helene, even
though I know this was all meant to be and that we each played
our necessary roles, I need you to forgive me for the times I hurt
you and for the ways I acted out. I am so sorry that you were hurt
by me. Please forgive me." It didn't occur to me to have her seek
my forgiveness, but it was vital to my soul's peace that I ask for
hers, even knowing it had all been for a higher purpose.

Helene responded, "Of course I forgive you, Michael. I understand, and I am sorry for hurting you so deeply. Please forgive me. It is so good to see you. Thank you."

I cannot describe the relief and joy I felt with this woman with whom I had spent three years while we had taken turns breaking each other's hearts.

With our arms around each other, we walked to the table to join the collection of characters who had played such significant roles in our past-life drama. Everyone was there: our old lovers, neighbors, business associates, children, ministers, rabbis, and even best friends who had turned betrayers. Everyone who mattered was present. The whole cast then laughed and reminisced about how we had befriended, betrayed, and supported each other at various times in our individual life dramas. Some of these individuals were people whom I swore I never even wanted to breathe the same air with again, and yet here we were, congratulating each other on roles well-played. It was a celebratory cast party at the Cosmic Lounge.

I awakened suddenly from that intensely vivid dream with tears running down my cheeks. I sat up in bed and said out loud to no one, "That's it! That's it! That is how it really is." I was free at last—free to let the drama go and to move on. In that moment of crystal clarity, I knew life was all about unconditional love and forgiveness, even though there was really nothing to forgive, and it was about seeing the perfection of the bigger picture.

For the first time, I was genuinely able to forgive myself, Helene, and all those seeming "villians" who had invaded our play in that past life. I saw them all as actors who had agreed to play different roles in each other's lives so we could learn the lessons necessary to grow our souls. Some of them were truly gifted! As usual, Shakespeare was right when he penned, "All the world's a stage. And all the men and women merely players; They each have their exits and entrances; And one man in his time plays many parts…"

It was after having that breakthrough dream that I was able to release my resentment toward Helene and forgive myself for being a less-than-noble partner in that relationship. I was determined to do it differently next time. Shortly thereafter, I met and fell totally in love with the woman who would become my best friend, lover, partner in ministry, wife, and teacher of compassion, Faith Moran. We were together for twenty-seven rich years. Everything I learned about myself during my exciting and bumpy adventure with Helene had prepared me for whom and what was to follow. What followed was so fulfilling, it was far beyond my ability to comprehend. I now know that it could not, nor would not, have happened without everything that preceded it. Thank You, God!

Years later, I told Faith about the dream and how I clearly saw that everything happens for a reason, and everyone who crosses our path does so by Divine Appointment. It is up to each of us to find, or sometimes assign, meaning and purpose to whatever life brings us. We both accepted this, and whenever we encountered one of *those* people or situations that totally confounded us, we would look at each other with raised eyebrows and say, "Well, I wonder how this one will play out in the Cosmic Lounge." And then we moved on with life.

"This being human is a guest house. Every morning, a new arrival. A joy, a depression, a meanness, some momentary awareness comes as an unexpected visitor. Welcome and entertain them all! Even if they are a crowd of sorrows, who violently sweep your house empty of its furniture, still treat each guest honorably. He may be clearing you out for some new delight. The dark thought, the shame, the malice, meet them at the door laughing, and invite them in. Be grateful for whoever comes, because each has been sent as a guide from beyond."

Rumi

Isaiah 58: 9–12

While in ministerial school and shortly before we were to be ordained, Faith and I were asked to select a scripture upon which our ministry would be built. When Faith and I found this one, we knew at once that Isaiah 58:9–12 was it.

Isaiah 58: 9-12*
⁹ Then you shall call, and the Lord will answer;
You shall cry, and He will say, "Here I *am*."
If you take away the yoke from your midst,
The pointing of the finger, and speaking wickedness
¹⁰ *If* you extend your soul to the hungry
And satisfy the afflicted soul,
Then your light shall dawn in the darkness,
And your darkness shall be as the noonday.
¹¹ The Lord will guide you continually,
And satisfy your soul in drought,
And strengthen your bones;
You shall be like a watered garden,
And like a spring of water, whose waters do not fail.
¹² Those from among you
Shall build up the old wasted places;
You shall raise up the foundations of many generations;

And you shall be called the repairers of the breach,
The restorer of streets to dwell in.

*New King James Version

Notes

Chapter 4: Muller, Wayne. *A Life of Being, Having, and Doing Enough.* New York: Harmony Books, 2010. Print.

Chapters 3 and 17: Ruiz, Miguel. *The Four Agreements: A Practical Guide to Personal Freedom.* San Rafael, Calif.: Amber-Allen Pub. 1997. Print.

Chapter 49: [1]Centers for Disease Control and Prevention. "Morbidity and Mortality Weekly Report," 1997, 46:101–105

Resources

Association for Global New Thought
www.agnt.org

www.dailyword.com
Daily Word, A Unity® Publication, offers insight and inspiration
to help people of all faiths live healthy, prosperous and meaningful lives. Subscriptions are available in print as well as online, by
email and on your smartphone.

Oneness Ministries was created to foster peace and mutual
respect among world religions and spiritual traditions through
education, the promotion of universal ethical standards, and
cooperative service projects. www.OnenessMinistries.com

Join Michael Moran on group experiences to spiritual places
throughout the world.
www.OnenessTravels.com

Unity stands for peace in the presence of conflict, love in the
presence of hatred, forgiveness in the presence of injury. Unity
honors the many names for God, the many paths to God, the
many ways to worship God, for there is only One Presence and
One Power, and that God loves each of us equally.

It is therefore the position of Unity Worldwide Ministries and the Unity Institute and Seminary to urge all nations, their leaders, and their people to turn to God, by whatever the name, for guidance during these challenging times and pursue peace, not war, for this is what honors the God of all our faith traditions. Unity stands for peace in our lifetime.

Silent Unity Prayer
www.unity.org/prayer/request-prayer
For more than 120 years, Silent Unity has been praying with and for people throughout the world.
Call: 1-800-NOW-PRAY (669-7729)

Spiritual Life Center in Sacramento, California, is an Interfaith Unity Ministry weaving ancient spiritual traditions with emerging wisdom. www.SLCworld.org

Unity Institute and Seminary
www.unityinstitute.org

Unity Worldwide Ministries
www.unityworldwideministries.org

About the Author

Michael Moran is a lifetime peace and civil rights activist, Interfaith Unity Minister, author, and student and teacher of interfaith studies. In 2012 he was recognized for his activism when he was presented the Gandhi, King, Ikeda Peace Builders Award by the Dr. Martin Luther King Jr. International Chapel at Dr. King's alma mater, Morehouse College in Atlanta, GA.

Michael and his late wife, Faith, believed that interfaith education and cooperative service projects were the paths to a lasting world peace. They actively embraced the belief held by Hans Kung, Mahatma Gandhi, and Dr. King that there will never be peace on earth until there is peace and harmony among the religions of the world. Together they were recognized with the Spiritual Leadership Award, the Building Unity Award, The Voice of Unity Award, The Father Louie Vitale Interfaith Award, and The Charles and Myrtle Fillmore Awards.

Michael and Faith were chosen by the late humanitarian artist, Isaac Soltes, to carry on his work by producing and distributing the original Oneness Symbol which has been called the Peace Symbol of the 21st Century. This beautiful symbol is worn or displayed by thousands of people worldwide as a beacon of hope and possibility for peace among world religions.

www.OnenessMinistries.com

Made in the USA
San Bernardino, CA
20 September 2013